TRIBES

by Nina Raine

(in order of appearance)
Daniel **Harry Treadaway**
Beth **Kika Markham**
Christopher **Stanley Townsend**
Ruth **Phoebe Waller-Bridge**
Billy **Jacob Casselden**
Sylvia **Michelle Terry**

Director **Roger Michell**
Designer **Mark Thompson**
Lighting Designer **Rick Fisher**
Sound Designer **John Leonard**
Casting Director **Julia Horan**
Assistant Director **Monique Sterling**
Production Manager **Tariq Rifaat**
Stage Manager **Laura Flowers**
Deputy Stage Manager **Nicole Keighley**
Assistant Stage Manager **Laura Draper**
Costume Supervisor **Jackie Orton**
Rehearsal Signer/Communication Support **Lucy Scott**
Voice Coaches **Jessica Higgs & Bardy Thomas**
Video Designer **Jack James**
Stage Management Work Placement **Francesca Ponsonby**
Set Built and Painted by **Souvenir Scenic Studios Ltd**

The Royal Court and Stage Management wish to thank the following for their help with this production: Access to Work, Deafinitely Theatre, English National Opera, Graeae Theatre Company, Charmian Hoare, the Lyric Hammersmith, MacColl Media, Pascale Moroney, Nadia Nadarajah, Puretone Ltd, Remark! Training, Royal National Theatre, Deepa Shastri, Alison Wherry-Alimo.

THE COMPANY

NINA RAINE (Writer)

THEATRE INCLUDES, AS PLAYWRIGHT: Rabbit (Old Red Lion/Trafalgar Studios/59East59, New York); The Drunks – adaptation (RSC).

AWARDS INCLUDE, AS PLAYWRIGHT: 2006 Evening Standard Award for Most Promising Playwright; 2006 Critics' Circle Award for Most Promising Playwright.

FOR THE ROYAL COURT, AS DIRECTOR: Shades, Behind the Image Rough Cut.

OTHER TRHEATRE INCLUDE, AS DIRECTOR: Unprotected (Liverpool Everyman/Traverse); Rabbit (Old Red Lion/Trafalgar Studios/59East59, New York); Vermillion Dream (Salisbury Playhouse); Eskimo Sisters (Southwark).

AWARDS INCLUDE, AS PLAYWRIGHT: 2006 Best Director TMA Award, 2006 Amnesty International Freedom of Expression Award.

Nina's commission for Hampstead Theatre, Tiger Country, is due to be produced in 2011, she is also under commission with Out of Joint. Nina trained as an assistant director at the Royal Court under the Channel Four YRTDS scheme where she assisted the directors Dominic Cooke, Ian Rickson, Katie Mitchell, David Hare, James Kerr and Stephen Daldry.

JACOB CASSELDEN (Billy)

THEATRE INCLUDES: The Vagina Monologues, Ghost Sonata (Reading Animal Productions); Danny Diva (Manchester Royal Exchange/Soho); The Second Nature (QEH, Bristol); Suave Desert (Ladybrain); Romeo and Juliet, Normal (Off the Road); Be There (Deafinitely Theatre); Being Deaf is Bad for Your Health (Sign Charity); A Doll's House, Electra (Bath Theatre Royal); Tommy – The Who (Bristol Hippodrome); Pistol and Pansies (Handprint Theatre Company).

TELEVISION INCLUDES: Resistance, Soundproof, Blue Nectar, The Secret Garden, Casualty, Alien Empire, Pride & Prejudice, 50-50, 60, Ahead.

RICK FISHER (Lighting Designer)

FOR THE ROYAL COURT: Sugar Mummies, A Number, Far Away (& NY Theatre Workshop), My Zinc Bed, Via Dolorosa (& Broadway), The Old Neighborhood, Fair Game, Hysteria, The Changing Room, Rat in the Skull (Royal Court Classics), King Lear, Six Degrees of Separation (& Comedy), The Queen and I (& Vaudeville), Serious Money, Bloody Poetry, Three Birds Alighting on a Field, A Mouthful of Birds.

OTHER THEATRE INCLUDES: The Fantasticks (Duchess); Rope (Almeida); The Fastest Clock in the Universe (Hampstead); An Inspector Calls (Novello, London/Broadway); Billy Elliot (London/Australia/Broadway); Much Ado About Nothing (Singapore); The Family Reunion, Betrayal, The Philanthropist, Old Times (Donmar); The Cherry Orchard (Chichester Festival Theatre); Sweeney Todd (Gate, Dublin); Landscape with Weapon, Honour (National); Resurrection Blues (Old Vic); Tin Tin (Barbican); Jerry Springer the Opera, Blue/Orange (National/West End); Disney's The Hunchback of Notre Dame (Berlin); Matthew Bourne's Swan Lake (London/Los Angeles/Broadway/world tour).

OPERA INCLUDES: Salome (Japan); Madame Butterfly, Albert Herring (Santa Fe); The Tsarina's Slippers (Royal Opera House); Turandot (English National Opera); Peter Grimes (Washington); Betrothal in a Monastery (Glyndebourne/Valencia); Billy Budd, Radamisto, La Bohème, Daphne, Tea, Peter Grimes, Madame Mao (Santa Fe); The Fiery Angel, Turandot (Bolshoi); A Midsummer Night's Dream (La Fenice); Wozzek (Royal Opera House); Gloriana, La Bohème (Opera North); The Little Prince (Houston/New York/San Francisco/Batignano).

JOHN LEONARD (Sound Designer)

THEATRE INCLUDES: The Master Builder, Yes, Prime Minister, Cyrano de Bergerac, Calendar Girls, The Cherry Orchard, Taking Sides, Collaborations (Chichester Festival Theatre); The Silver Tassie (Druid, Galway/tour); Ceiling/Sky (Theatre Royal, Stratford East/Barbican); True West (Sheffield Crucible); London Assurance, The Power of Yes, England People Very Nice, Much Ado About Nothing, The Enchantment (National); Measure for Measure, Rope, Waste, Duet for One, The Homecoming (Almeida); The Gigli Concert, The Cripple of Inishmaan, Long Day's Journey Into Night (Druid, Galway/Dublin/New York/tour); Restoration, A Month in the Country, People at Sea (Salisbury Playhouse); The Glass Menagerie (Gate, Dublin); Carrie's War, Duet for One, In Celebration, Kean, Donkey's Years, Summer and Smoke, Glengarry Glen Ross (West End); Translations (Princeton/Broadway); Leaves, Empress of India, The Druid Synge (Druid, Galway/Dublin/Edinburgh/Minneapolis/New York).

AWARDS INCLUDE: John is the recipient of Drama Desk and LDI Sound Designer of the Year awards and Honorary Fellowships from the Guildhall School of Music & Drama and the Hong Kong Academy of Performing Arts.

KIKA MARKHAM (Beth)

FOR THE ROYAL COURT: Time Present (& Duke of York's), Twelfth Night, Shelley.

OTHER THEATRE INCLUDES: Women, Power and Politics (Tricycle); The Permanent Way (Out of Joint/National); Julius Caesar, Homebody/Kabul (Young Vic); The Vagina Monologues (Ambassadors); A Wedding Story (Soho/UK tour); Song at Twilight (Guildgud); The Country Girl (Greenwich); Real Writing (Riverside Studios); Black Sail, White Sail (Gate); The Flag (Bridge Lane); A Bright Room Called Day (Bush); The Taming of the Shrew (Theatre Clywd/West End); Blow on Blow (Soho Poly); Macbeth, Anthony and Cleopatra (Haymarket); The Taming of the Shrew (Royal Lyceum, Edinburgh); The Seagull (Nottingham Playhouse).

TELEVISION INCLUDES: Einstein and Eddington, Party Animals, Lord Longford, Messiah, The Line of Beauty, Dirty Filthy Love, Born and Bred, Canterbury Tales: The Man of Law's Tale, The Forsyte Saga, Inspector Lynley Mysteries, Waking the Dead, Touching Evil, The Woman in White, Trial and Retribution, Kavanagh QC, Takin' Over the Asylum, Cracker, The Bill, Chronicles of the Young Indiana Jones, The Good Guys, A Woman at War, Poirot, Van Der Valk, Arms and the Man, Return of Sherlock Holmes, Black Silk, Blade on a Feather, Edward & Mrs Simpson, Clouds of Glory, Double Dare, The Basement.

FILM INCLUDES: Franklyn, Paint It Yellow, The Fever, Esther Khan, Killing Me Softly, Wonderland, A Very British Coup, The Innocent, Outland, Anne and Muriel, Operation Outbreak, Blood of Hussein, Nor Oit.

AWARDS INCLUDE: Clarence Derwent Award, Best Supporting Actress for Song at Twilight.

ROGER MICHELL (Director)

FOR THE ROYAL COURT: My Night with Reg, The Key Tag, The Catch, The Morning Show, Archangel Michael (& Sheffield Crucible).

OTHER THEATRE INCLUDES: Rope (Almeida); The Female of the Species (Vaudeville); Betrayal, Old Times (Donmar); Landscape with Weapon, Honour, The Homecoming, Under Milk Wood, The Coup (National); Blue/Orange (National/West End); Some Sunny Day (Hampstead); Some Americans Abroad (Lincoln Center, New York); Marya (Old Vic); Redevelopment, Restoration, Two Shakespearean Actors, Conversation, Kissing the Pope, The Constant Couple, Hamlet, Temptation, The Merchant of Venice, The Dead Monkey (RSC); Macbeth (Nuffield, Southampton); The White Glove (Lyric Hammersmith); Romeo and Juliet (Young Vic); Private Dick (Lyric Hammersmith/West End); La Musica, Off the Top, Small Change (Brighton Actors Workshop).

FOR THE ROYAL COURT, AS ASSISTANT DIRECTOR: Eclipse, Happy Days, Inadmissible Evidence, Wheelchair Willie.

FILM & TELEVISION INCLUDES: Morning Glory, Venus, Enduring Love, The Mother, Changing Lanes, Notting Hill, Titanic Town, My Night with Reg, Persuasion, The Buddha of Suburbia, Downtown Lagos.

DOCUMENTARIES INCLUDE: Michael Redgrave; Ready When You Are, Mr Patel (BBC Omnibus).

MONIQUE STERLING (Assistant Director)

FOR THE ROYAL COURT, AS ASSISTANT DIRECTOR: Spur of the Moment.

OTHER THEATRE INCLUDES, AS DIRECTOR: In the Solitude of Cotton Fields (The Clare, Young Vic);   A Certain Child (Michael Frayn Studio); Mystical Awakening Extravaganza (BAC); Tuesday (Soho Studio); Ache (Baron's Court); Dinner Party (George Wood).

OTHER THEATRE INCLUDES, AS ASSISTANT DIRECTOR: Young NHS project (The Clare, Young Vic); Troilus and Cressida (Shakespeare's Globe); Tunnel 228 (Punchdrunk/Old Vic/Young Vic); Betting on the Dust Commander (Albany); The Worth of Thunder (Soho Studio); 2008 Schools Festival (Young Vic).

Monique is Trainee Director at the Royal Court, supported by the BBC writersroom.

MICHELLE TERRY (Sylvia)

THEATRE INCLUDES: Light Shining in Buckinghamshire (Arcola); London Assurance, All's Well That Ends Well, England People Very Nice (National); Love's Labour's Lost (Shakespeare's Globe); 50 Ways to Leave Your Lover, The War on Terror, Two Cigarettes (Bush); The Man Who Had All The Luck (Donmar); The Promise (New Wimbledon); A Winter's Tale, Pericles, Days of Significance, The Crucible (RSC); Beautiful Thing (Sound Theatre, London); The Burial at Thebes (Nottingham Playhouse); As You Like It (Newcastle-under-Lyme); Blythe Spirit (Bath Theatre Royal/tour/West End).

TELEVISION INCLUDES: Reunited, Law & Order, Extras.

AWARDS INCLUDE: 2008 Manchester Evening News Theatre Award for Best Actress in a Visiting Production for The Man Who Had All the Luck.

MARK THOMPSON (Designer)

FOR THE ROYAL COURT: Piano Forte, The Woman Before, Wild East, Mouth to Mouth, Neverland, Six Degrees of Separation, Hysteria, The Kitchen.

OTHER THEATRE INCLUDES, AS DESIGNER: La Bête (West End/Broadway); London Assurance, England People Very Nice, The Rose Tattoo, The Alchemist, Once in a Lifetime, Henry IV Part I and II, The Duchess of Malfi, What the Butler Saw, Pericles, The Day I Stood Still, The Madness of George III, The Wind in the Willows (National); Life x 3 (National/Old Vic/Broadway); Arcadia (National/Lincoln Center NY); God of Carnage (Gielgud, Broadway); The Female of the Species (Vaudeville); Joseph and the Amazing Technicolor Dreamcoat (Adelphi); Kean (UK tour/Apollo); And Then There Were None (Gielgud); Funny Girl (Chichester Festival Theatre); Mamma Mia! (Prince of Wales/Prince Edward/Toronto/US tour/Broadway/Japan/Germany/Australia); Bombay Dreams (Apollo Victoria/Broadway). Costumes for Uncle Vanya and Twelfth Night (Donmar Warehouse/B.A.M.); Measure for Measure; The Wizard of Oz; Much Ado About Nothing; The Comedy of Errors; Hamlet, The Unexpected Man (RSC); Insignificance, Company, The Front Page (Donmar); The Blue Room (Donmar/Broadway).

OTHER THEATRE INCLUDES: The Lady in the Van (Queen's); Dr Dolittle (Hammersmith Apollo); Blast (Hammersmith Apollo & Broadway); Art (Wyndham's & Broadway). Set only for Follies (Broadway).

OPERA INCLUDES: Carmen (L'Opera Comique); Macbeth, Queen of Spades (Metropolitan Opera, New York); Falstaff (Scottish Opera); Peter Grimes (Opera North); Ariadne auf Naxoœ (Salzburg); Il Viaggio a Reims (Royal Opera House); Hanseland Gretal (Sydney Opera House); The Two Widows (ENO). Costumes only for Montag Aus Licht (La Scala, Milan).

BALLET INCLUDES: Don Quixote (Royal Ballet).

FILM INCLUDES: Costume design for The Madness of King George.

AWARDS INCLUDE: Mark is the winner of 4 Olivier Awards and 2 Critics Circle Awards.

STANLEY TOWNSEND (Christopher)

FOR THE ROYAL COURT: The Alice Trilogy, Shining City, The Weir (& Duke of York's/Australian tour), Under the Blue Sky.

OTHER THEATRE INCLUDES: Phèdre, Gethsemene, Happy Now, Guys and Dolls, Remember This, The Little Clay Cart (National); Art (West End); Who Shall Be Happy? (Mad Cow Productions); The Gingerbread Mix-Up (Andrew's Lane, Dublin); Amphibians (Dublin Festival); The Wake, Trinity for Two, Sacred Mysteries (Abbey, Dublin); Prayers of Sherkin (Old Vic); Who Shall Be Happy? (Mad Cow, tour); Pride and Prejudice, Oleanna, The Dream, The Double Dealer, The Cherry Orchard (Gate, Dublin); Democracy (Bush); Speed-the-Plow (Project Arts); Someone to Watch Over Me (West Yorkshire Playhouse); The Plough and the Stars (Young Vic); Saint Oscar (Field Day); Sexual Perversity in Chicago, The Caucasian Chalk Circle, The Country Wife, Nightshade, The White Devil (Rough Magic); I Can't Get Started (Dublin/Edinburgh Festival).

TELEVISION INCLUDES: Zen, Shadowlane, Ashes to Ashes, New Tricks, Whistleblowers, He Kills Coppers, Prosperity, Tribe, Rough Diamond, Hustle, Waking the Dead, Spooks, Elizabeth the Virgin Queen, Omagh Bombing, The Brief, Murder Squad, Fallen, Wire in the Blood, The Commander, Seventh Stream, Menace, Heartbeat, Station Jim, Table 12, Casualty, Best of Both Worlds, Active Defence, DDU, Ballykissangel, Peak Practice, Jonathan Creek, A Touch of Frost, Career Opportunities, Bliss, The Governor, The Bill, Parnell, Nighthawks, Fortycoats, Lost Belongings, Lapsed Catholics.

FILM INCLUDES: Killing Bono, Station Jim, Water's Rising, Happy-Go-Lucky, The Tiger's Tale, Flawless, Nativity, The Libertine, Mystics, Suzie Gold, Wonderous Oblivion Isolation, Inside I'm Dancing, The Tulse Luper Suitcases, Part II, American Girl, Monsieur N, Mystics, The Van, My Friend Joe, Moll Flanders, Jake's Progress, Beyond Reason, Good Girls, In the Name of the Father, Blue Ice, Into the West, The Miracle, Taffin.

Stanley is a founding member of Rough Magic Theatre Company.

HARRY TREADAWAY (Daniel)

FOR THE ROYAL COURT: Over There (& Schaubühne, Berlin), The Libertine (Royal Court 50th, reading).

OTHER THEATRE INCLUDES: Ghosts (West End).

TELEVISION INCLUDES: The Shooting of Thomas Hurndall, Cape Wrath, Recovery, Miss Marple.

FILM INCLUDES: The Last Furlong, Albatross, Pelican Blood, Fish Tank, City of Ember, The Disappeared, Control, Brothers of the Head. Short: Love You More.

PHOEBE WALLER-BRIDGE (Ruth)

THEATRE INCLUDES: Like A Fishbone (Bush); Rope (Almeida); 2nd May 1997(nabokov/Bush); Roaring Trade (Paines Plough/Soho); Crazy Love (Paines Plough); Is Everyone OK? (nabokov).

TELEVISION & FILM INCLUDES: How Not to Live Your Life, The Reward.

THE ENGLISH STAGE COMPANY
AT THE ROYAL COURT THEATRE

'For me the theatre is really a religion or way of life. You must decide what you feel the world is about and what you want to say about it, so that everything in the theatre you work in is saying the same thing … A theatre must have a recognisable attitude. It will have one, whether you like it or not.'

George Devine, first artistic director of the English Stage Company: notes for an unwritten book.

photo: Stephen Cummiskey

As Britain's leading national company dedicated to new work, the Royal Court Theatre produces new plays of the highest quality, working with writers from all backgrounds, and addressing the problems and possibilities of our time.

"The Royal Court has been at the centre of British cultural life for the past 50 years, an engine room for new writing and constantly transforming the theatrical culture." Stephen Daldry

Since its foundation in 1956, the Royal Court has presented premieres by almost every leading contemporary British playwright, from John Osborne's Look Back in Anger to Caryl Churchill's A Number and Tom Stoppard's Rock 'n' Roll. Just some of the other writers to have chosen the Royal Court to premiere their work include Edward Albee, John Arden, Richard Bean, Samuel Beckett, Edward Bond, Leo Butler, Jez Butterworth, Martin Crimp, Ariel Dorfman, Stella Feehily, Christopher Hampton, David Hare, Eugène Ionesco, Ann Jellicoe, Terry Johnson, Sarah Kane, David Mamet, Martin McDonagh, Conor McPherson, Joe Penhall, Lucy Prebble, Mark Ravenhill, Simon Stephens, Wole Soyinka, Polly Stenham, David Storey, Debbie Tucker Green, Arnold Wesker and Roy Williams.

"It is risky to miss a production there." Financial Times

In addition to its full-scale productions, the Royal Court also facilitates international work at a grass roots level, developing exchanges which bring young writers to Britain and sending British writers, actors and directors to work with artists around the world. The research and play development arm of the Royal Court Theatre, The Studio, finds the most exciting and diverse range of new voices in the UK. The Studio runs play-writing groups including the Young Writers Programme, Critical Mass for black, Asian and minority ethnic writers and the biennial Young Writers Festival. For further information, go to www.royalcourttheatre.com/ywp.

"Yes, the Royal Court is on a roll. Yes, Dominic Cooke has just the genius and kick that this venue needs… It's fist-bitingly exciting." Independent

ARTS COUNCIL ENGLAND

Supported by
ARTS COUNCIL ENGLAND

PROGRAMME SUPPORTERS

The Royal Court (English Stage Company Ltd) receives its principal funding from Arts Council England. It is also supported financially by a wide range of private companies, charitable and public bodies, and earns the remainder of its income from the box office and its own trading activities.

The Genesis Foundation supports the Royal Court's work with International Playwrights. Theatre Local is sponsored by Bloomberg. The Jerwood Charitable Foundation supports new plays by new playwrights through the Jerwood New Playwrights series. £10 Monday Nights is sponsored by French Wines: Wines of Quality. The Artistic Director's Chair is supported by a lead grant from The Peter Jay Sharp Foundation, contributing to the activities of the Artistic Director's office. Over the past ten years the BBC has supported the Gerald Chapman Fund for directors.

FOR THE ROYAL COURT

Artistic Director **Dominic Cooke**
Deputy Artistic Director **Jeremy Herrin**
Associate Director **Sacha Wares***
Artistic Associate **Emily McLaughlin***
Diversity Associate **Ola Animashawun***
Education Associate **Lynne Gagliano***
Producer **Vanessa Stone***
Trainee Director **Monique Sterling**‡
PA to the Artistic Director **David Nock**

Literary Manager **Christopher Campbell**
Senior Reader **Nicola Wass****
Literary Assistant **Marcelo Dos Santos**
Studio Administrator **Clare McQuillan**
Writers' Tutor **Leo Butler***
Pearson Playwright (The John Mortimer Award)
Alia Bano

Associate Director International **Elyse Dodgson**
International Projects Manager **Chris James**
International Assistant **William Drew**

Casting Director (Maternity Cover) **Julia Horan**
Casting Director **Amy Ball**
Casting Assistant **Lotte Hines**

Head of Production **Paul Handley** #
Acting Head of Production **Tariq Rifaat**
Acting JTU Production Manager **Matt Drury**
Production Administrator **Sarah Davies**
Acting Head of Lighting **Stephen Andrews**
Acting Lighting Deputy **Katie Pitt**
Lighting Assistant **Jack Williams**
Lighting Board Operator **Jack Champion**
Head of Stage **Steven Stickler**
Stage Deputy **Duncan Russell**
Stage Chargehand **Lee Crimmen**
Chargehand Carpenter **Richard Martin**
Building & Productions Assistant **Jerome Jones**
Head of Sound **David McSeveney**
Sound Deputy **Alex Caplen**
Sound Operator **Helen Skiera**
Head of Costume **Iona Kenrick**
Costume Deputy **Jackie Orton**
Wardrobe Assistant **Pam Anson**

Executive Director **Kate Horton**
Head of Finance & Administration **Helen Perryer**
Planning Administrator **Davina Shah**
Senior Finance & Administration Officer
Martin Wheeler
Finance Officer **Rachel Harrison***
Finance & Administration Assistant **Tessa Rivers**
PA to the Executive Director **Caroline Morris**

Head of Communications **Kym Bartlett**
Marketing Manager **Becky Wootton**
Press & Public Relations Officer **Anna Evans**
Communications Assistant **Ruth Hawkins**
Communications General Assistants
Kimberley Maloney, James McPhun
Sales Manager **Kevin West**
Deputy Sales Manager **Daniel Alicandro**
Box Office Sales Assistants **Cheryl Gallacher,
Ciara O'Toole, Helen Murray***, **Natalia
Tarjanyi***, **Amanda Wilkin***

Head of Development **Gaby Styles**
Senior Development Manager **Hannah Clifford**
Trusts & Foundations Manager **Khalila Hassouna**
Development Manager (Maternity Cover)
Lucy Buxton
Development Assistant **Penny Saward**
US Fundraising Counsel **Tim Runion**
General Fundraising Assistant **Beejal Pandya**

Theatre Manager **Bobbie Stokes**
Deputy Theatre Manager **Daniel O'Neill**
Duty Managers **Fiona Clift***, **Claire Simpson***
Events Manager **Joanna Ostrom**
Bar & Food Manager **Sami Rifaat**
Bar & Food Supervisors **Ali Christian,
Becca Walton**
Head Chef **Charlie Brookman**
Bookshop Manager **Simon David**
Assistant Bookshop Manager **Edin Suljic***
Bookshop Assistant **Vanessa Hammick** *
Customer Service Assistant **Deirdre Lennon***
Stage Door/Reception **Simon David***, **Paul
Lovegrove, Tyrone Lucas**

Thanks to all of our box office assistants, ushers and bar staff.
On sabbatical
** The post of Senior Reader is supported by NoraLee & Jon
Sedmak through the American Friends of the Royal Court Theatre.
‡The post of the Trainee Director is supported by the BBC
writersroom.

* Part-time.

TRIBES

Nina Raine

To Pat, and Jules

Characters

CHRISTOPHER, *Billy's father. Fifties/sixties*
BETH, *Billy's mother. Fifties/sixties*
RUTH, *Billy's sister. Twenties. The middle child. A year or two
    older than Billy*
DANIEL, *Billy's brother. The oldest child. Twenties. A year or
    two older than Ruth*
BILLY, *twenties. The youngest child. Deaf*
SYLVIA, *twenties. Going deaf*

Setting

Present day

Author's Thanks

With thanks to William L Ager, Cathy Woolley, Abbie Willis, all
at Mary Hare School, particularly Karen Smith, Nicolas and
Maya Slater, Penny Levy, Robert Skinner, Jodee Mundy,
Oliver Westbury, James Kearney, Jeremy Herrin,
Roger Michell, Dominic Cooke, St John Donald and my family,
especially Moses. And thank you to all those who helped me
understand what it was like to be deaf but don't wish to be
named. You know who you are and I am very grateful to you.

*The characters and events depicted in this play are fictitious. Any
similarity to actual persons, living or dead, is purely coincidental.*

Key to Notation

Italic bold type indicates dialogue that is signed, silently, and surtitled. (And, in the case of Act Two, Scene Two *only*, silent subtext that is surtitled.)

A forward slash (/) in the text indicates the point at which the next speaker interrupts.

A forward slash at the start of a line indicates simultaneous speech.

This text went to press before the end of rehearsals and so may differ slightly from the play as performed.

ACT ONE

Scene One

Black. In the black, the hum of an orchestra tuning up. A few strings at first, then more and more instruments, until the whole orchestra is alive. Just as the noise builds to its climax:

Lights up on a dinner table and family dinner in progress. Noise. There is a piano in the room. Two chaotic and noisy conversations mid-flow between DANIEL *and* BETH, *and* RUTH *and* CHRISTOPHER. BILLY *sits eating in silence.*

DANIEL. These nuts are *all* rotten.

BETH. They're from the garden.

CHRISTOPHER. He's a *cunt*.

RUTH. No, he's *not*.

DANIEL. I know they're from the garden. I've cracked about *forty* and not one of them is edible.

CHRISTOPHER. He's sixty. He's too old for you.

RUTH. Sixty's not old.

BETH. I'm sixty.

CHRISTOPHER. I know you're sixty. *I'm* sixty and *I'm* fucking old and so are you.

BETH. Have you finished your pasta?

CHRISTOPHER. We're both old. Yes. I have finished my pasta. I'm not eating it. What the hell did you put on it?

BETH. Smoked roe.

CHRISTOPHER. It's like being fucked in the face by a crab.

DANIEL. Did you know he's never forgiven his dad for circumcising him?

CHRISTOPHER. *Brilliant!* That is wonderful.

RUTH. What's so bad about that?

CHRISTOPHER. 'What's so bad about that?'? Every time he takes his cock out for a pee, he *hates* his father. Fantastic!

DANIEL (*rejecting a nut*). *Another* one!

BETH. You *are* boring. I got them off the lawn, they're absolutely fine.

DANIEL. Right, the ones even the squirrels wouldn't eat.

RUTH. There *are* quite a few rotten ones –

CHRISTOPHER. He's full of that post-colonial *horse-shit* –

BETH. Here! Here's one that's okay. Here you go.

CHRISTOPHER. 'You say something nice about my book and I'll say something nice about yours.' The coral-reef school of criticism. They all stick together.

DANIEL. Oh, thank you. It's perfect. Almost. 'Ambassador, you spoil us with your rotten nuts.'

CHRISTOPHER. Are you making fun of your mother?

DANIEL. In a nutshell, yes.

CHRISTOPHER. I won't have it. – He married some dusky lady. Then he ran off with another one. He's a potato-nosed cunt. I just can't believe you're going to fall for that… *bagel*.

BETH (*re:* CHRISTOPHER). He's got a good word for everyone.

RUTH. Well he was *nice* to me.

CHRISTOPHER. Bet he was.

RUTH. He seemed interested in what I had to say.

DANIEL. Well, you know what they say. 'There's no such thing as a boring fanny.'

RUTH. Oh, fuck you.

BETH (*to* RUTH). Where did you meet him?

RUTH. Natalie's christening. I was singing. It was full of people wandering around –

DANIEL. – Thinking 'What the fuck am I doing here?'

CHRISTOPHER. He's a drunk, and a womaniser.

BETH. That's not fair, Christopher. He's trying to get a new post.

DANIEL. So now he's teetotal, and impotent.

BETH *has got up, touches* BILLY*'s arm.* BILLY *turns to face her.*

BETH. Have you had some nuts, Billy?

BILLY *shakes his head, goes back to his plate of food.* CHRISTOPHER *carries on talking.*

CHRISTOPHER. You should read his fucking book.

DANIEL. Oh, shut *up*, Dad.

CHRISTOPHER (*getting up, going out, shouting from off*). I'm going to go and get it. Read you a sample sentence. That'll put you off him.

DANIEL (*shouting, to* CHRISTOPHER). Why don't you care who *I* fall for?

CHRISTOPHER (*shouting, from off*). Because you're my son, not my daughter.

DANIEL (*to* BETH). Is that why she got a brace? Why didn't *I* ever get a brace?

RUTH. Because they loved me, and they didn't love you, that's why you have promiscuous sex, and hate me…

BETH (*mildly*). Don't be silly. – Daniel, you need to clear your stuff out of Billy's room, now he's back.

RUTH. Yeah, Dan. You have a truly epic amount of porn.

DANIEL. I need the space!

CHRISTOPHER (*coming back in, he flicks around and reads from the book*). '…Narrative is phallic.' 'The thetic, or mirror stage of development is Lacanian, where the semiotic self becomes coherent and acquires language' – so before you look in the mirror, you're just a jigsaw having a nervous breakdown – 'Without language – '

He is cut off by an outburst of impatience from DANIEL *and* RUTH *in unison –*

DANIEL. / We get it, we get it –

RUTH. / All *right* –

CHRISTOPHER. ' – Without language our thought will die.' I thought *I* was going to die. (*Snapping the book shut.*) Has Billy got his aids in?

BETH. Yes.

CHRISTOPHER. Billy. (*He touches* BILLY*'s shoulder.*) Sweetheart. Are they on? (BILLY *nods.*)

BETH. I thought it was interesting.

CHRISTOPHER. Christ, *did* you?

BETH. By the time you got to the end of it.

CHRISTOPHER. But how did you stay *alive* till then?

DANIEL (*brandishing a huge carton of orange juice*). Why do we buy everything *sumo*-sized in this house?

DANIEL*'s mobile phone rings. In the course of* CHRISTOPHER*'s next sentence,* DANIEL *answers it.*

CHRISTOPHER. Who doesn't like orange juice? No one in the whole fucking world, that's who.

DANIEL (*into the phone, sunnily*). Hi. No, hi, we were just arguing.

He heads out of the room, on the phone.

CHRISTOPHER. Billy! Welcome back! –

DANIEL (*exiting*). Hang on – no reception.

CHRISTOPHER. – Join in! Have an argument!

(*In an undertone, re: the phone call.*) Was that her?

BETH. Yes. I think they're back on.

CHRISTOPHER. Christ. (*To* RUTH.) Is he smoking pot again?

RUTH. Dunno.

CHRISTOPHER. Which means 'yes', obviously. Fucking stupid. When's he going to move out again? Why am I surrounded by my children again? When are you all going to fuck off?

BETH. Billy's only just got back from uni –

CHRISTOPHER. I'm not talking about Billy, Billy's a pleasure, I'm talking about – (*He indicates* RUTH.) the parasites, you and Dan. Hurry up and start writing novels.

(*Opening up a laptop on the table.*) Now.

There is uproar from BETH *and* RUTH.

BETH. / For God's sake, Christopher.

RUTH. / Dad, *no*.

CHRISTOPHER (*ignoring them*). Now, let's see.

RUTH (*to* BETH, *getting up in protest*). I thought we made a rule!

BETH. It's incredibly boring for the rest of us.

RUTH. If you're doing it, I'm leaving.

The noise of a Chinese lesson starts up from the laptop, underscoring the following dialogue: a series of phrases in Chinese, followed by commentary in English. BILLY *turns to* RUTH *and* BETH. *He speaks in a slightly 'deaf' voice.*

BILLY. What are you talking about?

RUTH. It's like having a *telly* on the table!

BETH. We only come together once in the day –

RUTH. And no one else can speak!

CHRISTOPHER. How else am I going to learn?

RUTH. Do it in your study. Not here!

BILLY. What are you all *talking* about?

In the sudden stand-off as CHRISTOPHER *and* RUTH *eyeball each other, the Chinese lesson fills the room.*

CHINESE SPEAKER 1. *Ni hui shuo Zhongwen ma?* ['Can you speak Chinese?']

CHINESE SPEAKER 2. *Hui shuo yidian.* ['Just a little.']

CHINESE SPEAKER 1. *Ni lei ma?* ['Are you tired?']

CHINESE SPEAKER 2. *You yidian lei.* ['A little bit.']

DANIEL *comes in, hears the Chinese.*

DANIEL. Oh, *God.*

Another silence, filled by the sound of the Chinese lesson – now, the commentary in English.

COMMENTARY. In this dialogue, we have the expression '*you yidian*': 'a little bit'. '*Yidian*' is usually used after the verb, for example, *'Ta hui shuo* yidian *Yingwen –* '

DANIEL *steps forward.*

DANIEL. Well – I *have* to listen to this.

He grabs a radio, dumps it on the table. He hastily flicks through a cacophony of channels until he finds what he is looking for: Radio One. 'Bohemian Rhapsody' booms out, reaching its climax, clashing with the Chinese lesson. Everyone listens in silence. CHRISTOPHER *does nothing. 'Bohemian Rhapsody' comes to an end. The Radio One DJ cuts in.* BETH *stands up, snaps the radio off.*

BETH. Honestly, Daniel.

Silence.

COMMENTARY. '*Yingwen –* '

CHRISTOPHER *snaps his laptop shut, picking it up, dignified, and leaves the room.*

Silence.

BETH. Well! Thank you very much.

DANIEL (*in an undertone*). Prick.

Silence.

BETH (*to* RUTH). Help me clear.

RUTH. I *hate* us all living here again!

They start to clear the table of nutshells, plates, etc. In silence. They take them from the dining room, to the kitchen, offstage. DANIEL stays, standing. He sits, sighs, groans, puts his head on the table.

BILLY (*to* DANIEL). What happened?

DANIEL (*to himself*). Nothing.

Nothing…

(*He makes an effort, lifts his head so BILLY can see his lips.*) Dad was being annoying. Again.

He gets up, walks out. BILLY is left alone at the table. Silence.

We hear BETH and RUTH's voices, offstage.

BETH (*off*). No, you can leave that. It's just rubbish. Leave it.

RUTH (*off*). Shall I throw it away?

BETH (*off*). Yes. Throw it away.

Silence as BILLY sits at the table. Lights dim slightly, except on BILLY. BILLY stares into space.

DANIEL comes back in, stands in the doorway. He is on his mobile again, but not talking, just listening to the person at the other end of the line. He makes to speak, doesn't, shifts from foot to foot, but stays in the same place, at a distance from BILLY. Finally –

DANIEL (*crestfallen*). Oh… I see… Yeah…

…Alone… Yeah.

BILLY stares out. We no longer hear DANIEL's voice, although he continues to talk into the phone. Music builds. 'Overture' from The Magic Flute, *one and a half minutes in.*

Scene Two

BETH *sits with* DANIEL *in the kitchen. She is bent over his bare foot.* DANIEL *has a sheaf of notes in his hands and he is reading aloud from them, summarising the argument. Music fades.* BILLY *sits quietly nearby, reading.*

BETH. Dad is much better at this.

DANIEL. ... Ultimately, language is worthless.

BETH. Maybe if I used a needle... I think it might be a bit of *glass*...

DANIEL. Mum, *please* –

BETH. Go on, I'm listening.

DANIEL. We're prisoners of our own subjectivity. The subjectivity of our own perceptions.

BETH. – Dan, have you moved your stuff out of Billy's room yet?

DANIEL (*exploding*). Christ! There's a whole different set of bloody rules!

BETH. Dan – !

DANIEL. – Well, it's true! It would suit Dad just fine if Billy *never* left home, doing the frigging garden for him, but *we're* endlessly nagged –

BETH. Dan, this *isn't* about you moving out, you're shifting the parameters of the argument, *again*! I'm just saying, get your *stuff* out of Billy's *room*.

DANIEL. Why?

BETH. Because he needs his space, he's back now. You've got a perfectly good room of your own and you've colonised his with your crap. Anyway, I'm not discussing it. (*She indicates the fact that* BILLY *is in the room.*)

... Go on, I'm listening.

DANIEL. I'm not saying it all again.

> …Language is radically indeterminate. Language doesn't determine meaning. We have words but they are token, they are a pale photocopy of life. Ow!

BETH. Sorry.

DANIEL. That fucking hurt.

BILLY. What are you talking about?

DANIEL. My thesis. (*He goes back to his notes*.) How can you convey a nexus of feelings with words. – Don't *jab* it like that!

BETH. How did you *get* it, anyway?

DANIEL. I have no idea. It was just suddenly *there*.

> *Faintly, we hear the instrumental intro to 'Mon cœur s'ouvre à ta voix', which underscores the next few lines. DANIEL looks sharply at BILLY. BILLY is now staring into space.*

(*To* BILLY.) What's up?

> *Beat.*

Billy?

BILLY. What?

DANIEL. Is something up with you?

BILLY. No. Nothing.

DANIEL. You keep staring into space.

BETH. You *are* very quiet today, Billy. Is something the matter?

> *RUTH comes in, holding her laptop, from which 'Mon cœur…' is playing, and the volume of the aria increases correspondingly. She puts down the laptop.*

RUTH. Mum, I need your help.

DANIEL. Oh, for Christ's sake – (*Putting his hands over his ears*.) We're in the *middle* of something here!

RUTH. So I see; Mum's doing your splinter, waiting on you *literally* hand and foot. (*To* BETH.) I've Googled it, but it's all come up in French. (*Reading off the screen.*) '*Redis a mon tendresse*' – can you translate?

DANIEL. Godawful *warbling* –

BETH (*she gets up to look at the screen*). 'My heart', er… hold on… can we turn it down… (*She fruitlessly taps at the volume.*)

DANIEL. Just what we need – a musical fucking *interlude*!

RUTH. I've been *waiting*. For a pause in the bullshit. But there hasn't been one!

DANIEL (*gesturing at the laptop*). It just makes me feel *depressed*. It fills me with a deep depression.

RUTH. I know how you feel. 'Language is worthless, language is worthless.' Could hear it all the way upstairs.

BETH (*she has succeeded in turning it down*).

> 'My heart opens to your voice,
> Like the flowers to the dawn,'

– Erm, not sure what the next bit means.

DANIEL. It doesn't mean anything. It means 'ahh-ih-ahhih-aaa!' That's what it *means*.

RUTH (*to BETH, gesturing to DANIEL*). Mum – tell him to stop. He's been like this ever since I started getting gigs.

DANIEL (*pointing at her with his bare foot*). 'Gigs'! It was a fucking church hall. You're not Mick Jagger.

RUTH. I am Mick Jagger. Thirty-five people came.

DANIEL. Yeah, and you'll be swanning around for the next *week, enamelled* with triumph! (*He gestures at the laptop.*) Am I the only one that's noticed she can't go anywhere without a soundtrack suddenly?

RUTH *stares at him coldly.*

You are not in a film! You are not *Amelie*!

BETH (*appeals to both of them*). You are not in competition with each other!

DANIEL. It'll be like that *Aida* in the pub all over again. The one where the lighting was so dim I thought I'd finally gone blind from wanking. Togas, mottled arms, scary teeth and what they did with their *faces* –

BETH. They did very well, Dan.

DANIEL. No, they didn't.

BILLY (*to* DANIEL). Why are you upset?

DANIEL. Why would you do opera in a pub? I'll tell you why. Because you are minging! *That's* why!

RUTH. Well. That's me told.

BETH (*abstractedly, studying the screen*). Daniel's not upset… Let me see if I can find a translation.

BILLY. He's upset.

RUTH. He's being a cock.

DANIEL (*brightly*). Maybe Ruth *is* in a film. (*He sings.*) 'Ooh I'm the king of the jungle, the jungle VIP… '(*He makes some ape noises.*) 'Arh arh arh arh arh-arh… and that's what's botherin' me!'

RUTH *dismissively turns her back on* DANIEL *to look at the laptop over* BETH*'s shoulder.*

…Oh, put us out of our misery. Go well last night, did it? The 'gig'? Like one long blowjob? Audience like it?

RUTH. Since you ask, yes, they did.

DANIEL (*nodding*). They swallowed.

RUTH (*exploding*). Fuck you!!

BETH (*abandoning the laptop*). *Why* is there suddenly an argument?

BILLY *goes over, looks over* BETH*'s shoulder, takes the laptop from her, starts to scroll.*

RUTH. I'm fed up with him *baiting* me –

DANIEL. I'm fed up with her *enamel* of triumph –

BETH *puts her head in her hands*.

BETH. Why do you keep using this *phrase*, Daniel –

DANIEL. Because I think it's very accurate!

RUTH. I thought language was worthless!

DANIEL. When are you going to realise perfect pitch doesn't mean you've got a personality?

RUTH. You know, Dan, I used to really like you –

DANIEL. Oh, please, you've been saying that since you were *five* –

RUTH. – But you've become a real shit! Just because *Billy* puts up with it –

BILLY *has been scrolling on the laptop and suddenly interrupts*.

BILLY. 'The blossoms tremble on the gentle breeze,
    So does my heart tremble,
    Longing for your voice to come to me,
    How dear your voice is to me.'

Beat.

RUTH (*going over to* BILLY, *wonderingly*). Cool!

BILLY. Aria website.

BETH. Oh, well done, Billy!

BILLY. What's it about?

BETH (*to* BILLY). Delilah is seducing Samson. (*In a French accent.*) 'Sahn-sonne.' (*She scrolls.*) Delilah's a Philistine, so she's on the other side.

DANIEL. Oh my God, you're not going to sing it in *English*, are you?

RUTH (*flaring up*). Why else do you think I wanted the fucking translation?!

DANIEL. It's *fridge* poetry! 'Slumber,' 'tremble', 'ecstasy' – (*He sings a cappella.*) 'I have sucked a thousand cocks – '

BETH. *If* you're going to argue, slow down! (*She gestures at* BILLY.)

RUTH (*to* BILLY). You are not missing out on *anything*, Billy! (*To* DANIEL.) Text, subtext! Ironies! Layers! You've got to follow the story as well as the music so you get the irony, because she's *faking* –

DANIEL. Sorry, you're going to have to say all that again. Something about your voice, I just stopped listening.

RUTH. *Arse!!*

CHRISTOPHER *has come in, starts getting himself a drink.*

BETH (*to* CHRISTOPHER, *calmly*). They are arguing. About opera.

CHRISTOPHER. Oh God. I'm not getting involved. (*To the company at large.*) Maria Callas lugging her tits around the universe, or Janis Joplin: Janis every time. (*To* DANIEL, *noting his one clothed foot.*) And stop stealing my socks! You rip them with your horrible big toes! If you're going to live here, buy your own!

BETH (*to* DANIEL). But what's great about opera is it creates *feelings*, that, that you can't put into words –

CHRISTOPHER. *Bollocks,* we don't know what feelings *are* until we put them into words!

BETH. I thought you weren't getting involved!

CHRISTOPHER (*about to continue, he breaks off, baffled, looking at the carton in his hand*). – Why have we bought pear juice instead of orange juice?

BETH (*inflamed*). For a *change*!

CHRISTOPHER. Why? Pear juice is horrible! It's full of bits of grit, grit and… *tennis* court. (*To* RUTH.) *That's* the whole point of art. Putting feelings into words so that we know how to feel them.

DANIEL. Opera is a bunch of people listening to something they don't understand, feeling vaguely emotional and pleased with themselves. It's a bit like being *pissed*.

RUTH. – 'Ooh, look at my *essay,* look at my *idea* I found in my *pocket,* it's covered with bits of fluff, it's a bit old and lots of other people have already *licked* it but –

DANIEL (*losing his temper completely, he simply imitates the pitch of* RUTH*'s voice*). Neh neh neh! Neh neh neh!

RUTH. That's not –

DANIEL. Neh neh neh!

RUTH. – a very –

DANIEL. Neh neh neh!

RUTH. – effective way of arguing!

CHRISTOPHER (*amused*). Actually, it is.

DANIEL *seats himself at the piano, starts to crash out inversions.*

DANIEL. Listen to me! Listen to me playing inversions! Let's invert the chord! Look, I'm musical too! G at the top! A at the top! C at the top! That's what it's like in this family! Who's on fucking top!

Meanwhile, BILLY *has got up, and suddenly puts his arm around* DANIEL.

BILLY (*loudly*). It's all right, Dan.

The jangling chord DANIEL *was playing hangs in the air.*

Dan's upset.

BETH. Daniel?

DANIEL. No I'm not, Billy. I'm not upset.

... For Christ's sake... God... I'm not upset!

DANIEL *is suddenly at a loss. He gets up from the piano, unsteadily.*

CHRISTOPHER. What's going on?

DANIEL. Nothing.

He disentangles himself, wobbling on one foot.

This splinter is fucking killing me.

Pause. Suddenly, they all see that DANIEL *is close to tears. There is an uncomfortable silence.*

RUTH.... Sorry.

DANIEL *turns and walks out. Beat.*

CHRISTOPHER. Where the fuck did all that come from?

BILLY *speaks: his voice is starting to fragment a little, like a badly tuned radio – a sign that the batteries on his hearing aids are running down so he cannot monitor his own voice.*

BILLY. Told you he was upset.

Beat.

RUTH. Oh, God.

BETH. Ruth, you should be nicer to him.

RUTH. How was I to know!!

Beat.

BETH. It's hard for him living at home again.

RUTH. It's hard for *me* living at home again.

CHRISTOPHER. So why don't you both sod off?!

Beat.

Why the hell is he writing a *thesis*?

BETH. He wants to be an academic. –

CHRISTOPHER. Well he's not an academic. It's perfectly obvious what he should be: a stand-up comedian.

BETH. Oh for God's sake, Christopher.

CHRISTOPHER. His impressions are brilliant!

BETH. He doesn't want to *do* impressions! He wants to prove himself.

CHRISTOPHER. Who to?

BETH.... Himself.

CHRISTOPHER (*mystified*). *Why?*

>...Why doesn't he stick to the *funny* stuff? That's what he's good at.

BILLY. He's upset about Hayley.

RUTH. He's smoking pot.

CHRISTOPHER (*whispers*). Have you *read* his thesis? I started it. I couldn't finish it.

RUTH (*whispers*). Neither could I.

BETH (*whispers*). He's trying to find his voice!

CHRISTOPHER (*whispers*). Well, he's speaking in the wrong language!

>(*Abandoning the whisper.*) Why are we all whispering?

RUTH (*also in her normal voice*). I don't bloody know.

CHRISTOPHER. He needs to get a *job*.

BETH (*waving this aside, to* BILLY). He talks to you. What happened with Hayley?

BILLY (*indistinctly*)....Wha?

>CHRISTOPHER *gestures at* BILLY*'s aids*.

CHRISTOPHER. Bill. (*He enunciates, speaking loudly.*) Your voice. Going. Batteries on your hearing aids. Must be going.

BILLY. Oh. (*He fiddles with them.*)

RUTH (*enunciating*). *Hayley*. What did Daniel tell you?

BILLY (*indistinctly*). Nothing. I just saw it on his face.

>I think they've split up again.

RUTH. Oh, *God*.

BETH (*wearily*). Christ. Why can't you move a *step* without an argument starting in this house?

CHRISTOPHER. Because we love each other!

RUTH. Yeah. Like a straitjacket. (*She mimes being in a straitjacket.*)

DANIEL *comes back in, looking through an opera programme in his hand. Everyone physically – and infinitesimally – registers this.* RUTH *immediately sobers up.*

Daniel. I'm sorry if I offended you.

DANIEL (*ignoring her, riffling through the programme*). All right… *all right…* wait *just* a minute… (*He riffles more.*) Ah.

(*He finds the passage he wants and reads aloud triumphantly.*) 'When he accidentally tastes the dragon's blood spilt on his hands, *Siegfried* understands the song of a *woodbird*, who informs him of a mysterious woman asleep in a ring of *fire*.'

BETH (*soothingly*). Well, of *course* that's silly. It's Wagner.

RUTH *nods, wordlessly puts her hands up in agreement.*

CHRISTOPHER. Could be Terry Pratchett.

RUTH. Yep.

There is an uncertain pause.

CHRISTOPHER. Look, Daniel, as regards Hayley, you're well off out of it. Even if it does mean you have to live here again. After spending time with her, your IQ *visibly* halved.

RUTH (*nodding kindly*). It was like *possession*.

CHRISTOPHER. You were even starting to talk like her.

RUTH (*zombie-like, northern accent*). 'Hayley.' 'Hayley.'

CHRISTOPHER. Anyway, I'm not saying any more and neither should anyone else because you're probably going to get back together again.

DANIEL. And dilute your fucking *gene* pool. Let's face it, no one's ever going to be good enough for *this* family –

CHRISTOPHER. Look, between these four walls I'll have honesty! The girl was a northern twat, she had all the charisma of a *bus* shelter, she was as thick as two *tits*. She –

BETH. / Christopher –

RUTH. / Pa –

DANIEL. / Dad – *leave* it!

> CHRISTOPHER *mimes zipping his lips shut.* BILLY
> *gestures to the laptop again, raises his voice, which is
> fragmenting more.*

BILLY (*to* BETH). What happens in the story?

BETH. Delilah betrays him. I agree with Ruth, the music isn't
half so sad unless you know the story.

RUTH. *Thank* you.

> BILLY *suddenly stands up.*

BILLY. I've met someone.

> *Beat.*

I've met someone.

I've met this girl.

> *Silence. They all turn to stare at* BILLY.

BETH....Well, that's lovely!

DANIEL. What girl?

> BILLY*'s voice starts to fragment again.*

BILLY. She's going deaf. She comes from a deaf family. They
all sign. I met them.

BETH. When?

> *Pause.*

DANIEL. Have you kissed her?

RUTH. At last, a sensible conversation.

BILLY. She's got a boyfriend.

BETH. Oh.

> *Beat.*

What's her name?

BILLY. Sylvia.

Beat.

When BILLY *next speaks, his voice is fragmenting to the extent that what he says is not quite intelligible. It is like listening to someone on a mobile phone with poor reception – ends and beginnings of words.*

Wh-I met h-, so-thing – ju –

… fe – into – lace… here.

Beat.

CHRISTOPHER. Say again?

BILLY (*making an effort*). It was li… so-thi switched on… in my mind.

Pause.

CHRISTOPHER. His aids. Batteries going.

DANIEL. She reminded you of someone?

BILLY. I tho – she – the… nn.

BETH. Billy. Consonants.

Subtitles start to come up as BILLY *struggles, with ends and beginnings of words, and they look at him, uncomprehendingly.*

When I met her, something just clicked in my head.

BILLY. When I met her… something… jus… -lic… my head.

It was like a light being lit in my mind.

It was li… a ligh… be- li… in my mind.

I thought, she's the one.

I tho – she – the… nn.

I wanted to tell you.

I -anted to -ell you.

BILLY *falls silent. They look at him. Another aria has started to play, faintly, from* RUTH's *laptop. 'Porgi, amor'* (*from* The Marriage of Figaro), *in at the singing.*

DANIEL....You like her?

BILLY *nods, silently. They all look at him, in silence. The music swells. Black. Subtitles:*

> **'Oh love, bring some relief.**
> **To my sorrow, my sighs:**
> **Oh give me back my loved one.**
> **Or in mercy let me die.'**

Scene Three

DANIEL *is sitting in the kitchen. Night. He stares into space. Silence.*

BILLY *comes in, wearing his coat. He sees* DANIEL. *He is startled.*

BILLY. Hi... I just texted you... There was no reception there.

DANIEL. Right.

BILLY. I only just got it. Sorry.

DANIEL. It's okay.

> *Beat.*

BILLY. How come you're up?

> DANIEL *shrugs. He gets up, puts the kettle on. He turns back to* BILLY.

DANIEL. Couldn't sleep.

> Where were you?

BILLY. With Sylvia.

DANIEL. Where did you go?

> BILLY *doesn't answer.* DANIEL *clears the table, collecting papers off it. Reads from one.*

> (*To himself.*) 'Pamino has taken a vow of silence.'

BILLY. What?

DANIEL. Nothing.

> BILLY *sits at the table.* DANIEL *switches on the radio, stands, looking at* BILLY *while he waits for the kettle to boil: Bach's prelude in E-Minor is playing. Pause.*

BILLY. Dan… I'm feeling bad.

DANIEL. Why? No reason to feel bad. I just called you and you didn't answer. No reason to feel bad.

> *There is a moment while the music plays.*

BILLY.… Sorry… Dan… can you turn it off…

> DANIEL *looks at him.*

It just contaminates… It's just this buzz…

DANIEL. Sorry.

> *He turns it off.*

BILLY. It means I can't pick out what you're saying.

DANIEL. I wasn't saying anything.

> *Silence.*

BILLY.… Your face looks funny.

> *Beat.*

DANIEL. Someone's shouting my name.

BILLY. Like how?

DANIEL. Dan, Dan, Dan, Dan, Dan. Dan, Dan, Dan.

Like that. Pretty unimaginative.

BILLY. Right now?

DANIEL. That's why I switched the radio on.

Beat. The kettle has boiled.

BILLY. Do you know why it…

DANIEL. No. There's never any trigger.

BILLY. Did it wake you up?

DANIEL. No, I was already awake.

If I talk about it, it makes it worse.

Tell me about Sylvia.

Beat.

BILLY. Dan, who are the voices?

DANIEL. What?

BILLY. Who are the voices. Do you know them, I mean?

DANIEL. Dad. Mum. Sometimes Nana. Family, basically.

BILLY. What do they say?

DANIEL. That I'm wasting my life. That I'm a bad person. It's all quite limited and quite general. Probably because it's my subconscious that's coming up with it.

Beat. Then –

BILLY. / But is it –

DANIEL. / But they're –

Beat.

BILLY. Are they accurate?

DANIEL. Yeah, very accurate.

Beat.

It's quite personal and it's quite loud tonight.

I don't ever get you. Weirdly.

Pause.

You're thinking about her again, aren't you.

BILLY.… No.

DANIEL. I can see it on your face.

DANIEL *laughs affectionately,* BILLY *sheepishly.*

It's that fucking obvious. Silly Billy.

Beat.

You look happy.

BILLY. I'm sorry… I can't help it.

DANIEL. No. No, that's great. That's great.

Beat.

When are you going to let us meet her?

BILLY. Dan… all this week… I was trying to remember her
    face in my head. In the end, it was like I wore it out… like I
    photocopied it too many times.

DANIEL. Right.

Beat.

Has she dumped her boyfriend yet?

BILLY. …I don't know.

DANIEL. Right.

BILLY. Why do you keep saying 'right'…

DANIEL. No reason.

BILLY. What is it…

DANIEL. Look… I really don't want to piss on this, you
    know… I'm being honest with you now, Billy… But… It's
    like you've switched off your brain or something… these
    borrowed sort of emotions…

Sorry, however I say it, it's going to sound horrible.

I just don't want you to get hurt.

Just make sure you keep a little bit of yourself separate.

BILLY. What do you mean?

DANIEL. You give someone your heart and they leave it on the
    bus… and it gets trodden on. That's all.

Beat.

You know when people say 'I love you for yourself'?…
There's no such thing. Because you *are* how talented you
are, how quick you are, how clever you are. And then that
changes. Sometimes you're stupid. Love doesn't last. You
don't know what it's like.

Beat.

What? Don't look depressed. What's wrong? You've met
someone you like. Fantastic. At last.

Beat.

BILLY. I thought you'd be pleased.

DANIEL. I am pleased. It's fantastic. It's great.

Pause.

Can I put the radio on now? It helps me block them out.

BILLY *is still, watching* DANIEL. DANIEL *goes over to the
radio, switches it on again. Music plays, softly.* BILLY *turns,
looks down at his hands.* DANIEL *comes and stands behind*
BILLY, *unseen. He speaks.* BILLY *is oblivious.*

You know, whenever I dream about you you're always ten
years old.

Well done, Billy. Billy, Billy, Billy, Billy.

Music: 'Move Over' by Janis Joplin.

Scene Four

DANIEL *and* RUTH *in the kitchen.* RUTH *is preparing the
table for dinner. We hear muffled shouting from off. They both
look up above them.*

RUTH. The expression 'I feel low'… I *do* feel low, I want to
get down on the floor.

She lies on the floor.

It's going to be a disaster.

DANIEL (*speaking in a Geordie accent, mock voice-over style*). 'Ruth has been a heroin addict now for *thirteen years*. Today is an average day.'

RUTH (*interrupting, she looks at her watch*). Shut up. He's going to be here any minute and they're behaving like children. (*She sits up.*) And by the way, I want my fucking pen back, Dan. The red one.

DANIEL. Why *are* they arguing?

RUTH (*getting up from the floor*). Don't think I haven't noticed you took it. I'm warning you, that's my favourite pen, you thieving little shit. – I think it's about the novel. Dad read the first chapter, he doesn't like it.

CHRISTOPHER*'s voice floats down.*

CHRISTOPHER (*off*). *You* cannot *call the Iron Curtain the 'Ferrous Veil'! There is nothing naffer than titivating a cliché!*

BETH (*off*). *Oh, fuck you, Christopher!*

CHRISTOPHER (*off*). *You want to be a writer, you have to take criticism!*

BETH (*off*). *I am fed up with being shouted at!*

CHRISTOPHER (*off*). *Look, you've got a dedicated reader here –*

BETH (*off*). *Dedicated, my arse!*

The shouting moves off and becomes indistinct. DANIEL *and* RUTH *look at each other.*

RUTH. She said last night she doesn't know why they're still together.

DANIEL. Mind you, she is *inventively* pessimistic.

RUTH. Have *you* read it?

DANIEL. No. Apparently it's about a fucked-up family.

RUTH. God! Where did she get *that* from?

RUTH inspects a pile of books on the table, picks one up.

'*How to Mend a Broken Heart*'. I thought it was about a therapist.

DANIEL. Well, now it's about a marriage breakdown.

RUTH shifts the pile of books off the table. DANIEL turns back to his laptop.

RUTH. Don't, Dan!

DANIEL. Yeah, 'Don't, Dan!' I agree. (*Tapping at the laptop, shaking his head to himself.*) I'm young, I'm fertile, I should be lavishing this attention on the clitoris. Ah. Here we go. 'Lastdesperateattemptatthesis12.doc.'

... I can't believe the only people getting any sex in this house are over fifty. (*Shivering.*) And when are they going to mend the fucking central heating?

RUTH (*gloomily inspecting her reflection in a spoon*). I've got these *veins* on the side of my nostrils.

DANIEL. So have I. You can't do anything about them. We get them from Mum.

RUTH. ... I realised the other day. Dad's bored by me.

DANIEL. So? He's bored by me, too. He's got a very low boredom threshold.

RUTH. Right.

He looks at her, closely.

DANIEL. You're not going to *cry*, are you?

RUTH. No.

DANIEL. You *sure*?

RUTH. Yes! (*She gives a slightly wild laugh.*)

DANIEL. Is that 'the laughter to stave off tears'?

RUTH. No!!

Beat.

…Dad's bored by me, because what I do has nothing to do with writing.

DANIEL. At least he's not constantly nagging you to get a job.

RUTH. At least he notices you.

DANIEL. He notices *you*.

RUTH. Only when he disapproves of my boyfriends.

DANIEL. Well, that's because he loves you, isn't it?

RUTH. Abusively.

DANIEL. Well, abusive love's all that's on offer here. Better that, than settling for some guy who's six shades of beige.

RUTH. But *is* it? Got to get out… I feel like a fucking *bonsai* tree… (*Inspecting her reflection in the spoon.*) Bet *Billy's* getting laid. Apparently this chick's teaching him sign.

DANIEL. Teaching him *sign*? (*Abandoning the laptop.*) Jesus! *Why?*

RUTH. What's wrong with learning sign? I think it's sexy.

DANIEL *has sprung up and is pacing.*

DANIEL (*inflamed*). *Sign!!* Fuck! Why doesn't she bloody leave him alone? He's fine how he is! He's been fine all his life. Why do people always want to *change* other people? I mean, does he *want* to learn sign? Just because he's *deaf* –

RUTH. Jesus, Dan – !

DANIEL. He told me, he *hated* the deaf stuff he went to! That's why he avoids it! – Christ, it's so fucking conventional. Join the club… like a fucking religion… You're deaf so you've got to learn *sign*… Bossing him around!

RUTH. …. Don't start… and don't tell Dad… you know what he'll be like about it…

DANIEL. I'm not having him bullied! Don't get me wrong, I'm happy for him. I'm fucking happy he's found someone. At last. It's amazing. Well done. But I'm not having him being dominated. *Hectored*. That mustn't happen.

RUTH. Yeah. Only by you.

DANIEL. Look, he's deaf… he's been a bit sheltered… I'm just worried that, you know, the iron grip of a pussy…

RUTH. I know, I know… *Do* you think they're shagging?

DANIEL. Oh, God… Why did she have to be *deaf*… They're obviously a nightmare…

RUTH. Dan… shh… Anyway… He's doing better than us.

DANIEL. Nothing happening with old what's-his-face? You need to bug him. Persistence pays.

RUTH. Men can bug women. Not vice versa.

DANIEL. No, bollocks. You've got to bug him. You're obviously not bugging him. You're not a bugger. I'm going to have to train you up.

RUTH. How's Hayley?

DANIEL. Ah, fuck Hayley. (*He pats his pockets for cigarettes.*)

Suddenly BETH, *in trousers and a bra, storms through the room followed by* CHRISTOPHER. CHRISTOPHER *is holding a kimono.*

BETH (*inflamed*). Right! So we're back to *your* idea of me. Again. Well, you're welcome to it!

CHRISTOPHER. For Christ's sake!

BETH. You look at me and you see AGA Saga!

CHRISTOPHER. No I do not! You look nothing like –

BETH. Ha, ha, I'm sixty, so you think what I'm doing is *knitting*! Narrative scarf and *bootees* for my grandchildren – it's patronising!

CHRISTOPHER. *What* fucking grandchildren??!

BETH. Oh, for God's sake!!

BETH *exits out of the other door, followed by*
CHRISTOPHER. DANIEL *and* RUTH *look after them,*
wonderingly. Then RUTH *starts to chop up figs into*
quarters, DANIEL *takes over the preparation of the table, a*
cigarette now behind his ear.

DANIEL. I just want to know what he told her about *me*. I mean,
what's he told her? I *bet* he told her I was self-obsessed.

RUTH. Yeah. Ugh, a rotten one. Apparently she wanted to
know why *we'd* never learnt sign language.

DANIEL (*mystified*). Well why would we?? Why would we
learn sign language?

RUTH. For Billy.

DANIEL. None of her bloody business! Jesus. How come he's
been telling *you* all of this?

RUTH. He doesn't *belong* to you, Dan.

DANIEL. Yes, he does. He does belong to me.

    … I can tell I'm going to hate her.

RUTH. You don't know that. (*She looks at him.*) You might
love her.

    BETH *strides back into the kitchen, pursued by*
    CHRISTOPHER *in mid-flow.*

CHRISTOPHER. All I'm saying is, you've got to resist clichés!
It's sloppy and it's vague and you'll end up like that *Irish*
novelist – (*He speaks in a thick Irish accent.*) / 'Staves of
light fell across the *barn* – '

BETH. Patronising and, what is more, *snobbish*!

CHRISTOPHER. / It's the literary equivalent of *underscoring,*
it's poetic writing, it's 'fine writing', as in *Tesco's* Finest!

BETH. / Writing is not a hierarchy!

    (*With finality.*) – And I'm *not* going to wear the kimono!!

CHRISTOPHER. It is a beautiful piece of clothing.

BETH. It's completely unsuitable. I'm not going to wear it!

RUTH *suddenly interrupts.*

RUTH. 'Stop Arguing, Start Talking!'

CHRISTOPHER. Tell your mother she should wear the fucking kimono.

DANIEL. Don't wear the fucking kimono. You look silly.

BETH. The poor girl will –

CHRISTOPHER. Arh, Christ, who gives a toss about this fucking *girl*?! Can we have a little less *conventionality*, please!

DANIEL. Yeah! Wear the kimono, for God's sake!

BETH *holds up the kimono uncertainly.*

RUTH. It *is* really pretty, Mum.

BETH. I'm too old for it. (*To* RUTH, *imploringly.*) *You* wear it.

CHRISTOPHER. No! When you're old is *exactly* when you should wear a kimono! When you're old, and incontinent, I want you incontinent in a kimono.

CHRISTOPHER *embraces* BETH. *The tension is broken.*

BETH. I'm going to go up and get changed. They're going to be here in a minute. I suggest everyone pulls themselves together.

BETH *goes out, taking the kimono with her.*
CHRISTOPHER *looks at the table.*

CHRISTOPHER. Christ. What have you two been *doing* all this time?

DANIEL *and* RUTH *look at each other, speechlessly.*
CHRISTOPHER *starts to busy himself.*

Ruth – figs?

RUTH. Yes.

CHRISTOPHER. Put pepper on them?

RUTH. No.

DANIEL *puts his head in his hands histrionically.*

CHRISTOPHER. Dan. Wine.

RUTH. Were you arguing about the novel or the kimono?

CHRISTOPHER. Both. Get the pepper on those figs!

DANIEL. Why?!

CHRISTOPHER (*as if to an infant*). Putting pepper on figs brings out their flavour.

DANIEL *puts his head in his hands again*.

The kimono was the subtext, the novel was the context. Who laid *these* knives?

DANIEL. Me.

CHRISTOPHER. They're horrible!

DANIEL. It's a special occasion. We need horrible knives.

CHRISTOPHER *busies himself about the table, changing the knives*.

CHRISTOPHER. Well, I'm changing them. How deaf is she?

RUTH. Not as deaf as Billy but worse at lip-reading. Apparently.

CHRISTOPHER. Daniel, I see the greenhouse has basically become your ashtray.

DANIEL *puts his head in his hands again with a moan*.

Stop *doing* that! Either tell me to shut up –

DANIEL. Fine. Shut up.

CHRISTOPHER. Thank you. Stop smoking in the greenhouse.

DANIEL *pops a pill*.

DANIEL. And I'll take this antidepressant so I can get through the night.

CHRISTOPHER *goes out with the knives*.

RUTH. How are your voices?

DANIEL. I don't want to talk about them. Thanks.

Short pause. CHRISTOPHER *comes back in, with different knives.*

CHRISTOPHER (*surveying the table*). Right. Where am I going to put 'Sylvia'.

RUTH. Well, she'll need to be able to lip-read us all.

CHRISTOPHER. I'd better put 'Sylvia' and Billy separately. So they can't confer.

DANIEL. Yeah. She's making Billy learn sign. They'll probably start signing to each other.

CHRISTOPHER. What??

RUTH. Dan!

CHRISTOPHER. *Making* him learn sign?

BETH *comes back in, wearing the kimono.*

BETH. Yes, isn't it lovely? I was so pleased when I heard.

CHRISTOPHER. *Why?!* Fucking terrible idea! Next thing we know, he'll be banging on about the bloody deaf community!

BETH. What's wrong with that?

CHRISTOPHER. 'What's wrong with that?'? Defining your personality around the fact you're deaf, it's like basing your identity on coming from *Gateshead*! Or whether you support Arsenal! If what constitutes your identity becomes *ideological* –

RUTH (*to* DANIEL, *sarcastically*). Well done, Dan.

BETH. For God's sake, Christopher, he's learning it for *her*. It's got nothing to do with *Gateshead*! This is about him, and her, and nobody else. Can we all stop being so *possessive*? People do things for the people they love. (*She gestures irritably at the kimono she has on.*) Like me. Wearing a bloody kimono!

CHRISTOPHER. Exactly my point! It's like a marriage. It's not a marriage if it's open. Is it. 'Unless it's me and only me it's not love.' 'Forsaking all others.' Like any cult, it's founded on exclusion. A sect has to have enemies and –

BETH. '*Sect*'! For God's sake.

CHRISTOPHER. Okay. Maybe I shouldn't say sect. Cult? Is cult better? The feeling of persecution is *built in* –

BETH. Who are they persecuting?!

CHRISTOPHER. No, it's about *them* feeling persecuted.

BETH. *Who?*

CHRISTOPHER. The deaf! The fucking Muslims of the handicapped world. You feel like saying, take your hearing aids and shove them up your arse. The feeling of persecution is necessary because it *bonds* –

BETH (*interrupting*). Can we just leave it? Billy doesn't feel persecuted –

CHRISTOPHER. I'm not talking about Billy, Billy's not deaf –

RUTH *and* BETH (*in unison*). Billy *is* deaf –

CHRISTOPHER. He is not, he's been brought up in a hearing family, he's been protected from all that shit! I'm talking about the hardliners, capital-D deaf, not racists but *Audists* –

BETH. You have no idea if this girl is a hardliner or not! All he's doing is learning another language! You gave Hayley a hard time for being northern, and now you're giving this girl a hard time for signing! No one is ever good enough, are they!

RUTH. It's true, Dad, and it's very hard for us –

CHRISTOPHER. Making deafness the centre of your identity is the beginning of the end. Like being a *northerner*. Where your flaw is made part of your personality.

BETH. Christopher, what the hell has being a *northerner* got to do with anything?

RUTH. Because he's obsessed with it.

CHRISTOPHER. I am not! It's just obvious to me that no one in this house has anything in common with anyone who comes from Runcorn!

DANIEL. Except you, and the fact you were born there.

CHRISTOPHER. So I should know! I escaped.

BETH. So you'd exclude people who come from Runcorn from this house.

CHRISTOPHER. Yes, I bloody would. I've got no sentimentality about it. None.

DANIEL. As you told Hayley, at length, when *she* came round to dinner.

CHRISTOPHER. Hayley comes from Leeds, she needed to be told. And I enjoyed telling her. And, if you ask me, that's what *signing* is like. Northern.

RUTH. *Northern? Signing?*

BETH. My God, a confluence of *two* prejudices! Fantastic.

CHRISTOPHER. Yes. Northern. From what I can see. A lot of fake joviality. A construct of a personality.

DANIEL. Really? I always thought the signing persona was a bit *Jewish*. (*He does a bit of cod signing.*)

BETH. Dan. That is not nice.

DANIEL. We're Jewish, I'm allowed.

BETH. Just be nice to the poor girl, that's all I ask!

DANIEL. Yeah, let Sylvia get the same treatment as Hayley. Dad being 'nice'.

CHRISTOPHER. I refuse to be blamed for the fact that it didn't work out with that… bonobo.

BETH. Be quiet!

Beat. Everyone listens. The sound of keys in a door.

I think that was them.

CHRISTOPHER. It's okay. We can carry on. They're deaf.

BETH. They may be deaf. They're not stupid.

CHRISTOPHER. It is possible to be deaf *and* stupid, you know.

Just as he says this, BILLY *and* SYLVIA *walk in.* SYLVIA *is carrying a bunch of tulips.*

BETH. *Hello!*

> *There is a chorus of warm 'hello's all round.*

> DANIEL *and* SYLVIA *come face to face. There is a moment.*

SYLVIA. Hello.

DANIEL. Hello.

> SYLVIA *hands* DANIEL *the tulips.*

DANIEL. ...Thank you.

BETH. Well, Sylvia, it is lovely to meet you! (*Indicating her outfit.*) You may think this is a dressing gown, but you'd be wrong, it's a kimono.

CHRISTOPHER. Can I get you a drink? (*He moves* DANIEL*'s laptop.*) This is Daniel, who's writing a thesis that we all ironise... Red or white? Sit down, sit down. And Ruth, who sings...

SYLVIA. Sorry?

RUTH (*miming*). I sing.

SYLVIA. Oh, you're a singer?

RUTH. Well, a performer.

DANIEL. As of about three weeks ago.

SYLVIA (*to* RUTH). What kind of singing do you do?

DANIEL. The awful kind.

RUTH. Opera.

SYLVIA. That must be great.

RUTH. It is, I love it.

SYLVIA. What are you singing in at the moment?

DANIEL. The chorus.

RUTH. *The Magic Flute.* (*Enunciating.*) *The Magic Flute.* I'm in the, one of the sect, the Masonic...

DANIEL. Twats.

SYLVIA (*to* BETH). And you're a writer?

BETH. Yes. Late in life, but… I'm writing a detective novel.

RUTH. A *detective* novel?

BETH. Well. Why shouldn't I? It's a marriage-breakdown detective novel. I don't know who's done the murder yet. I'm going to decide at the end – (*She looks meaningfully at* CHRISTOPHER.) and then put all the clues in. That's what Agatha Christie did. (*To* SYLVIA.) I'm finding I'm having to do a lot of inventing.

CHRISTOPHER. No shit, Sherlock.

BETH (*with an edge to her voice*). And the thing I'm finding, it's all about empathy.

SYLVIA (*to* BETH). Sorry – what did you say?

BETH…. I was saying, I have to think myself into my characters' heads.

Beat.

SYLVIA (*to* DANIEL). Billy said you were writing something, too.

DANIEL. In a manner of speaking.

SYLVIA. So you're all…

CHRISTOPHER. Yes, terrible word, we try to avoid it, 'creative'.

RUTH. Apart from Billy. Thank God.

SYLVIA (*to* CHRISTOPHER). What do you do?

CHRISTOPHER. I used to teach. Now I write books.

Catching her look of incomprehension, he mimes, extravagantly, first 'scribbling', then 'typing', then 'reading'.

Books. Books.

SYLVIA. Oh! What sort of books?

DANIEL. The argumentative sort.

CHRISTOPHER. I think you mean critical.

DANIEL. No, I mean argumentative.

SYLVIA (*to* RUTH *and* DANIEL). You live at home as well?

RUTH. Yes, it's pretty unnatural, isn't it.

CHRISTOPHER. They tried the outside world and couldn't cope.

RUTH. You mean Daniel couldn't cope without Billy. Like the crocodile and the little bird that picks its teeth. What's it called?

DANIEL. Fuck off.

BETH (*overriding all this*). What do *you* do, Sylvia?

SYLVIA. I manage events for a charity – fundraising – DeafActs?

CHRISTOPHER. Ah, I *see*! A *deaf* charity?

BETH (*hurriedly*). And what lovely flowers!

She takes them from DANIEL.

Daniel, pour some wine.

She gives the flowers to RUTH.

Ruth, go and get a vase. Sylvia, are you vegetarian? Because I was going to make Cornish pasties –

CHRISTOPHER. Jesus! *Why?* If you eat more than one Cornish pasty you *die* of something, don't you? Cornishness, probably.

BETH (*to* SYLVIA). – But I've made steak and kidney pie.

CHRISTOPHER. Thank God. Have a fig.

He offers them to SYLVIA, *starts to eat one himself.*

DANIEL (*offering her wine*). Have some wine.

RUTH (*offering her nuts*). Pistachios.

CHRISTOPHER *bursts out coughing*.

Are you all right?

CHRISTOPHER. Sorry. (*Inspects the half-eaten fig in his hand*.)

BETH. All comes of putting pepper on one's figs. Stupid thing to do.

DANIEL (*to* SYLVIA). Are *your* parents this annoying?

SYLVIA. What?

BETH. I'm sorry, Sylvia –

SYLVIA (*loudly*). No, I got it… I get a lot… thank you…

There is a sudden pause.

DANIEL (*pointing at the two of them*). So… how did you and Billy meet?

SYLVIA…. Er… We met at an exhibition.

DANIEL (*sharply*). When? What exhibition?

BILLY. This deaf artist.

CHRISTOPHER. A deaf artist. Really. Any good?

SYLVIA. She's pretty untalented…

BILLY. We slagged off her work together.

DANIEL. Nothing more uniting for two people than bitching about a third.

CHRISTOPHER. Well, it's in us from the egg, isn't it. The playground. The essence of the club.

BETH (*to* SYLVIA). Yes, Daniel was bullied at school and –

DANIEL. Mum, I know you're desperate to make conversation, but don't start on that one. Pistachio?

SYLVIA *takes a pistachio. Her hand is shaking.*

SYLVIA. Sorry. My hand is shaking because I have an essential tremor. Not because I'm nervous. Although I am nervous.

BETH. No need to be nervous.

Beat.

We're all nervous.

CHRISTOPHER. Do you go to a lot of these deaf events, Sylvia?

BILLY. Yeah… with the job… Sylvia gets a lot of invites…

CHRISTOPHER. Do you like them? Deaf events? What's it like? The community?

SYLVIA. The community?

CHRISTOPHER. The deaf community.

(*Enunciating*.) The deaf community.

Beat.

SYLVIA. Erm… hierarchical.

BETH. No, Sylvia, he asked – (*She enunciates*.) 'What is the – '

SYLVIA. Yeah, I know.

It's hierarchical.

Beat.

RUTH. '*Hierarchical*'? How?

SYLVIA…. Well… I'm not deaf from birth so that makes me less good than someone who is. But I come from a very deaf family so that makes me more kosher. Billy's at the top of the pile because he's deaf from birth – like a cradle Catholic is better than a convert – but when he didn't know any sign, that took him down a few notches again.

RUTH. God.

SYLVIA. And everyone's slept with everyone.

CHRISTOPHER. Christ. That's very interesting.

… Isn't it a bit of a nightmare?

SYLVIA. It isn't that much fun being around hearing people any more, either. No offence.

DANIEL. Why not?

SYLVIA. Oh... the way they very politely let you know just how inconvenient it is. People yelling in your ear however much you explain, so you literally have to *grab* their face and stick it in front of you. And... they don't realise how obvious it is on their faces when they don't like you.

Beat.

CHRISTOPHER (*in an undertone*). I feel slightly ticked off.

There is a nonplussed pause.

Suddenly a mobile rings. BETH stands bolt upright, looks around for it in a panic.

BETH. Oh God –

DANIEL. Mum. Just because it rings –

BETH. – Where the hell is it...?!

RUTH. – doesn't mean you have to answer it.

BETH. Christ... Sorry about this... – Ah!

She locates it in her kimono pocket, plucks it out, looks carefully to see which button to pick up the call.

Hello?

Oh, hello... how *are* you!

...Really?!

A free kettle...!

On the word 'kettle', a dumbshow from the rest of the family starts up. CHRISTOPHER throws up his hands. RUTH makes retching gestures. DANIEL lets his head sink onto his knees. SYLVIA looks questioningly at BILLY. BILLY signs to her, unnoticed by everyone else, surtitled.

BILLY. *Cousin.*

BETH. Well, Zach, that sounds lovely. What fun! That sounds lovely. No, it really sounds lovely.

Oh, yes?

This weekend?

The dumbshow from the family is galvanised and becomes shaking heads, mouthed 'no's, throat-slitting gestures, etc.

Well… I'll have to ask Christopher, but –

– I'm going to say yes, Zach. Yes.

The family collapse in despair and give up on the dumbshow.

We would love to. Unless you hear from me again, it's a yes. We will. Okay, Zach. Much love to all of you. And I think that'll be lovely. Bye, Zach. Take care. Bye.

She uncertainly presses a button, double checks that the call is terminated, puts the phone down. Looks at the family. They look at her.

Oh God. I'm not sure I really want to do this.

The family explode.

DANIEL. / Why do you *do* it, Mum?

CHRISTOPHER. / *Why* did you agree to it??

DANIEL. Why did you keep saying 'lovely'?

RUTH. You said 'Take care'.

BETH. Did I? When did I say that? I *never* say that.

CHRISTOPHER. Sorry about this, Sylvia. Zach is –

BETH. No, I'm not having this. We spend our whole time being nasty about other people, it's cliquey and horrible and I'm not having it!

RUTH *goes and gets a vase, starts arranging the tulips in it.*

CHRISTOPHER. Why not? What's wrong with laughing at people? I think you should be able to laugh at *everyone*. I think Jews should be laughed at, I think the Irish should be laughed at, I think northerners should be laughed at, I think –

RUTH. Writers?

CHRISTOPHER. I think *everyone* should be laughed at – but *especially* if they believe in God! What I don't understand is why Zach's parents don't just *tease* him out of being kosher!

BETH. Because they don't want to be mean to their son!

CHRISTOPHER. Why not?

BETH. Because he's their son!

CHRISTOPHER. So what!

BETH. Why shouldn't he be religious? It's a scary universe out there. If you're part of a group, it's easier.

CHRISTOPHER. But that's exactly what you have to fight! *Don't* be part of the crowd! *If* someone laughs at a joke about George Bush, they've *got* to be stupid! (*Narrowly.*) Sylvia? What do you think?

SYLVIA. Er –

BETH. Don't bother answering him.

CHRISTOPHER. The majority is always *wrong*! Right?

DANIEL. / Ignore him.

CHRISTOPHER (*ignoring* DANIEL). / It all went wrong when Zach married that religious bird. And, like a fool, decided to procreate. Now, he's got the status of a pushchair. And what's he got in return? Rebecca.

RUTH. A very sadomasochistic violent relationship with bouts of amazing sex. Must try it some time. He has a gay walk. (*To* DANIEL.) Do the gay walk.

DANIEL. No.

CHRISTOPHER. That man redefines the meaning of the word 'uxoriousness'.

RUTH. What *is* the meaning of the word uxoriousness?

In quick succession.

DANIEL. / Wifely.

CHRISTOPHER. / Husbandly.

BETH. / Loving.

RUTH. Oh! I always thought it meant, sort of, 'over the top'.

DANIEL. In Zach's case, it does.

CHRISTOPHER. The fact is, Sylvia, Zach's wife, Rebecca –

BETH has her hand on CHRISTOPHER*'s shoulder and is warningly squeezing it.*

No, stop warningly squeezing my shoulder please, darling, I'm going with this – is a *supremely* – *unattractive* – lady. Why you would want to stick your cock into that *cement* mixer – stop squeezing my shoulder!

BETH. Christopher, stop it!

SYLVIA. Sorry, I didn't understand –

BILLY starts to sign rapidly to SYLVIA, *surtitled.* BETH *is the only one who notices.*

DANIEL. Cement mixer. It's a metaphor –

CHRISTOPHER. No, it's the / *truth* –

BETH. Look at Billy!

BILLY. *...He said fucking her must be like sticking your cock into a cement mixer.*

The others all stop and stare, fascinated.

SYLVIA. ... '*Cement* mixer'?

CHRISTOPHER (*wonderingly*). Yes...

Beat.

DANIEL. Dad likes using metaphors.

... Do it again? Billy?

BILLY. *He said fucking her must be like sticking your cock into a cement mixer.*

DANIEL. Wow.

Beat.

That was...

BETH. Really...

CHRISTOPHER. Yes. It really got a sense of Rebecca across.

Beat.

BILLY. Sorry... I just thought I'd translate as Sylvia's still...

DANIEL. No, that's great.

BILLY. To pick up.

DANIEL. Yeah.

Beat.

RUTH. Do you speak or sign with your parents?

SYLVIA. Sign.

Pause. She becomes self-conscious, turns to BILLY.

What did she ask, do I speak or sign with my parents?

BILLY. ***Yeah, that's right.***

(*To the family.*) You're going a bit too fast.

SYLVIA *turns back to the family.*

SYLVIA. Sorry... Because I was hearing... I'm not as good at lip-reading. I still get a lot. Vowels. The low frequencies. I can still *hear*. It just... doesn't make sense any more.

CHRISTOPHER. No, that's fine. Hayley could probably have done with an interpreter too.

RUTH (*enunciating*). Daniel's ex-girlfriend, Hayley. Daniel was going out with a girl with a huge conk.

SYLVIA. Huge *cock*?

CHRISTOPHER. *Conk.* (*Gesturing.*) Nose.

RUTH. Although Hayley probably had a huge cock too. Hayley was Dad, in a bra.

DANIEL *and* CHRISTOPHER. Fuck off!!

BETH (*musingly*). It's true. We all marry our parents. Or turn into them. (*To* RUTH.) You fall for dull men, who are versions of me. (*To* CHRISTOPHER.) And you've started whistling, like Grandpa.

CHRISTOPHER. I have not!

RUTH. Yes, you have, actually. You whistled three times yesterday.

CHRISTOPHER (*genuinely dismayed*). Did I? Christ.

Are you anything like your parents, Sylvia?

SYLVIA.... Do I like my parents?

CHRISTOPHER. No. *Are* you like your parents?

SYLVIA. Well... they're deaf... sorry, was the question...

Pause.

RUTH (*slowly*). Were your parents – are your parents deaf from birth?

SYLVIA. Yes.

Beat.

RUTH. And you're... going deaf?

SYLVIA. Yes... I'm turning into my parents.

There is an awkward ripple of laughter.

It's fine, I saw it happen to my brother first. When he was seventeen. Passed on... from our parents... There was a chance it wouldn't, but... genetic. It started a year ago now. Eventually, it'll all be gone. I'm not deaf yet, though. Just – in denial.

More laughter.

RUTH.... Can you say anything you like? In sign?

BILLY (*to* SYLVIA). You can. You're amazing at it.

SYLVIA. Billy...

CHRISTOPHER. I thought it was basically broken English.

BILLY (*signing to* SYLVIA). **Broken English.**

SYLVIA. No. It's got its own grammatical rules.

CHRISTOPHER. Like what?

SYLVIA. Oh… you know… you wouldn't say, 'Who's that fat man?', you'd say, 'Fat man – (*She points at* CHRISTOPHER.) who?'

Beat.

CHRISTOPHER. So it is broken English.

BILLY. No, it's not. Only if you translate it literally. If you translated any language literally it would sound like broken English.

CHRISTOPHER. So you can say anything? You can translate anything? Really?

SYLVIA. Yes. I think so.

CHRISTOPHER. How do you say… 'she's a bit of a moron.'

SYLVIA. *She's a bit of a moron.*

CHRISTOPHER. How do you say… 'she doesn't know what she's talking about.'

SYLVIA. *She doesn't know what she's talking about.*

CHRISTOPHER. How do you say… (*He speaks slowly and clearly.*) 'her mind's… like a… plastic bag… flapping… out of a car window.'

SYLVIA. Erm… *Her mind's like a plastic bag, flapping out of a car window.*

She turns to BILLY.

Is he trying to say something about me?

BILLY. *No. Don't be paranoid.*

CHRISTOPHER. What was that last bit?

Was it something about me?

BETH. Don't be paranoid.

Beat.

BILLY. You can say anything you want in sign. If you're as
good as Sylvia.

DANIEL. What about poetry? – Po-e-try?

SYLVIA.... Poetry? Oh, yeah. Of course.

DANIEL. Like what?

SYLVIA *looks at him.*

SYLVIA. Well – give me something to say.

Pause.

DANIEL. '... My heart is a boat on a rough, rough sea.

SYLVIA*'s hands move into the shape of a boat. Then, she
'bobs' the boat out and away from her body, towards*
DANIEL.

Headlong through space...

SYLVIA *makes the signs. They are expressive.*

From morn
To noon he fell, from
Noon to dewy eve...

SYLVIA (*recognising the poem*). Oh!

She makes the signs in tandem with DANIEL*'s speech. They
are as 'poetic' as the poetry.*

DANIEL.... a summer's day...'

Beat.

'My heart belongs to you...'

SYLVIA *looks at him. Clenches her fist in front of her chest.
Then presents it to* DANIEL.

DANIEL *stares at her.*

SYLVIA.... I thought everyone's parents spoke 'like that' –
(*She mimes signing.*) until I lost my mum at the supermarket
when I was five. Then I realised.

RUTH. Just like I thought everyone's parents walked round in
the nude shouting at each other.

SYLVIA.... They do.

BETH.... I taught Billy how to speak, Sylvia.

SYLVIA (*nodding*). When I first met him – Billy's lip-reading – I was amazed.

BILLY. Sylvia says I could use it. To get a job.

A pause while the family digest this.

DANIEL. What?

RUTH. How?

BILLY. Lip-reading for the Crown Prosecution Service. You look at CCTV for trials, you tell them what they're saying on the tape. It's a skill.

DANIEL *has turned so* BILLY *can't see his face.*

... Because I can do half face and even a bit of quarter face. Course it's easier if you know the person, but... she says I'm really good. And you get paid.

Then I could move out. Get a flat with Sylvia.

Beat.

BETH. What a wonderful idea!

DANIEL (*under his breath*). Wowee.

CHRISTOPHER. I see.

DANIEL *gets up and distances himself from the group.*

RUTH. But Billy's never had a job...

SYLVIA (*to* BETH). When I first met Billy, I didn't realise he was deaf, his lip-reading was so good.

CHRISTOPHER. Well, we didn't bring Billy up as handicapped. We brought him up as if he were hearing.

Beat.

Although, to be fair, some deaf people would say that that *is* bringing him up as handicapped.

RUTH. Dad. Don't stir.

DANIEL turns back at this.

DANIEL. No. They'd say being deaf isn't a handicap, it's being in a linguistic minority.

SYLVIA (*to* DANIEL). No, being deaf is a handicap.

DANIEL and SYLVIA stare at each other.

If you're going from hearing to deaf. Like I am. Life is worse deaf.

If you're deaf from birth, I think it might be different.

BETH. It's strange, because Billy's always been deaf, he can't really explain what it's like. Because he's *in* it.

DANIEL (*to* SYLVIA). But you're in both worlds.

Beat. He enunciates.

You're in both worlds.

SYLVIA. Well, it doesn't feel like that…

DANIEL. No, you're in a unique position.

Beat.

CHRISTOPHER. So if you're in both worlds, you can tell us which language is better.

SYLVIA. …What?

CHRISTOPHER. Which is better, sign or speech.

BETH. Why does one have to be *better*?

CHRISTOPHER. Because one of them *will* be. I mean, Sylvia. Be honest now. I mean, let's not be *pious*. Just for one second here.

BETH. No one's being pious –

CHRISTOPHER. I know, and that's good. We're all being very open and politically incorrect, and that's fantastic.

Beat. He speaks directly to SYLVIA.

What are the limitations of sign?

BETH. Who says –

CHRISTOPHER. Oh, come on, because it's *got* to! The
   hypothetical philosophical level. Isn't that hard to do in sign?

DANIEL. Or sarcasm. Isn't it hard to do sarcasm? Because it's
   all about tone of voice. Not tone of face.

Beat.

SYLVIA. Sign's very concrete. It –

CHRISTOPHER. So what if you want to say something that
   isn't concrete?

BILLY (*raising his voice*). Sylvia used to interpret and in the time
   it takes to say eight adjectives she can do forty-five in sign.

CHRISTOPHER. Aw, *bollocks*.

BETH. Christopher!

CHRISTOPHER. Yeah yeah yeah, I know the hype, but
   seriously –

DANIEL. We don't want to hear what sign *can* do. We want to
   hear what it can't.

CHRISTOPHER. That's right!

BILLY (*to* SYLVIA). *Did you understand?*

SYLVIA. *Yes, I understood what he said.*

   BILLY *makes to speak.*

CHRISTOPHER. I'm asking Sylvia, Billy. Let her answer.

Beat.

SYLVIA. The thing is… Sorry, I just feel a bit…

CHRISTOPHER. A bit what?

SYLVIA. No, I just feel a bit…

Beat.

   …disloyal.

CHRISTOPHER. Why?

Beat.

Don't worry. You can tell me to piss off, I won't get offended.

SYLVIA. I don't care if you do get offended.

DANIEL. Disloyal to whom?

Meanwhile SYLVIA *has turned and is signing to* BILLY.

SYLVIA. *He doesn't like me.*

BILLY. *They do. He does like you. This is his way of showing it. He only does this to people he likes.*

Simultaneously to their signing, BETH *to* CHRISTOPHER –

BETH (*in an undertone*). Christopher, stop it.

CHRISTOPHER (*in an undertone*). Stop what?

BETH (*in an undertone*). You might make her cry.

CHRISTOPHER (*in an undertone*). Of course I'm not going to make her cry. The last thing I want to do is to make her cry.

SYLVIA (*loudly*). No, it's okay. You can make me cry.

CHRISTOPHER (*mildly*). I'm not trying to make you cry, I'm having a conversation. That's what we do in this house.

RUTH *fans herself, starts taking her cardigan off.*

RUTH (*generally*). Phew! Is it just me, or is it really stressful in here? – I mean, hot in here. Hot.

DANIEL. Well, *I* think this calls for a nuit-grave.

BETH. Dan.

DANIEL (*to* SYLVIA). A cigarette. Family slang.

CHRISTOPHER. I've told you, Dan. You're not allowed in the house.

DANIEL. Everyone in this room is a smoker apart from Ruth, I'm lighting up.

(*He lights a cigarette. Then turns to* SYLVIA.) Sylvia. What do you do if you want to pose a hypothesis in sign?

SYLVIA.... Like what?

DANIEL. *If* I smoke this cigarette, my dad will get angry. If my dad asked you any more questions, you *would* get angry.

Beat.

SYLVIA. You can't say 'would' in sign. Or 'if'.

CHRISTOPHER. Aha, I see.

SYLVIA. But –

CHRISTOPHER. Right. So, no word for 'if' or 'would'. Because this is where it gets interesting. I do words, Sylvia, that's what I do.

RUTH. He's a slag for words.

CHRISTOPHER. And I would say that if your language is a bit black and white then it makes *you* a bit black and white. Because how can you feel a feeling unless you have the word for it?

Beat.

SYLVIA. Deaf people can be more honest.

CHRISTOPHER. More honest? Or more tactless?

SYLVIA (*raising her voice*). Are you asking me whether signing makes you a coarser person because signing is a coarse language? Whether deaf people are emotionally deaf as well, lack empathy?

BETH. No, he's not asking that.

Beat.

DANIEL. Yes, he is asking that.

BETH *and* RUTH. Dan!

DANIEL. Well, he *is*.

SYLVIA. Well then I'll be coarse soon.

Deaf people can be blunt and direct and tactless. And paranoid. It's true. I see it in my parents.

Beat.

RUTH (*in an undertone*). Well done, Dan.

BETH. To be honest, *you're* both being pretty coarse and tactless, Daniel. And Christopher.

Sylvia... They didn't mean to hurt you.

SYLVIA (*loudly*). Sorry, it upsets me because I'm going deaf and actually, you're talking about my family.

Silence. SYLVIA *is on the verge of tears and no one knows what to do.* BILLY *takes her hand.*

BETH (*whispers*). Oh dear...

Silence.

CHRISTOPHER. I'm sorry.

Beat.

We didn't mean to upset you, Sylvia.

BETH. We're all very pleased to meet you.

SYLVIA (*still struggling with tears*). Sorry... I just get very upset still.

BETH. ...Why? You've got this wonderful language.

RUTH. Yes. I bet you sign's better than words at high feeling.

DANIEL *has got up and is looking at* BILLY *and* SYLVIA *holding hands.*

DANIEL. Yeah. How do you know what the word 'love' means? What does it *mean* when you say 'I'm in love'?

DANIEL *picks up the vase of flowers and brings it over to* SYLVIA.

Your tulips have opened.

Pause.

SYLVIA. Well... you don't have to pin the emotion down to a word. (*She signs different 'emotions', surtitled.*) **Jealous... angry... upset... insecure... sorry...**

RUTH. So it's like music. Non-verbal but it gives you feelings.

Pause.

SYLVIA. I can't hear music any more.

... I recognise that it's music, but I don't *understand* it. It's just a roaring sound now.

Pause.

It's like laughing, shouting, crying... they all sound the same. Just a sort of roaring.

Beat.

BETH. There's no chance you'll get it back?

SYLVIA. No.

Silence. SYLVIA points to the piano.

Who plays?

DANIEL. All of us. Apart from Billy.

SYLVIA. I used to play.

Beat. SYLVIA lets go of BILLY's hand and leaves him, to go over to the piano. She sits down. She puts her hands on the keys. Then, hesitantly, she starts to play Debussy's 'Claire de Lune'. A couple of mistakes but holding the melody.

As SYLVIA plays, where the surtitles have been appearing, slowly the notation for the music fades up: as abstract bars of different colour at different heights according to the pitch of the note.

One by one the family approach and come to stand, at various distances from the piano in an improvised semicircle. Except for BILLY, who stays apart, at a slight distance from them all, watching. SYLVIA's playing increases in confidence. BILLY turns away.

DANIEL turns from the circle around SYLVIA. He looks at BILLY, who is looking out and away.

Lights fade.

End of Act One.

ACT TWO

Scene One

DANIEL *is sitting in the kitchen. Night. He stares into space. Silence.*

BILLY *comes in, starts to make a cup of tea.*

DANIEL. Hi.

BILLY. Hey.

DANIEL. Where is she?

BILLY. Gone up to take her contact lenses out.

DANIEL. Is she staying?

    BILLY *nods. Beat.*

    How do you talk when you're in bed?

BILLY. You sign in the dark. You feel each other's hands.

DANIEL. By the way. Mum and Dad said to ask, does she want to come to France with us.

BILLY. Cool.

DANIEL. It's a love-love relationship. She's done a lot better than Hayley, tell you that for free.

    Beat.

    By the way, it was Dad's birthday yesterday.

BILLY. Oh, shit.

DANIEL. Yeah, well.

    Beat. The kettle has boiled.

    Are you pissed off with me about something?

BILLY. No.

Beat.

DANIEL. So? How did it go?

BILLY. Oh – fine. I'd watched it about forty times, I knew it off by heart. They just asked me about one bit, when they talked about the gun. Was I sure I'd got what he was saying, even though the CCTV was quite blurry, and he had his hood up. That was it, it was over really quickly –

DANIEL (*interrupting*). How's Sylvia?

Beat.

BILLY. Sylvia?… She's… she's… yeah, she's good. We had a Chinese and…

DANIEL. Do you think you'll get married?

Pause.

BILLY. Dan… it's weird… it's like… there was an empty place at the table and she came and sat down in it. I was alone… and now I'm not.

DANIEL. Great.

Beat.

BILLY. I'm looking at another tape for them next week. Prison-visit conversation. They said their regular lip-reader couldn't work it out so they're passing it on to me. It's a big one this one. Apparently.

DANIEL. A big one. Woo.

BILLY. Yeah.

Beat.

A lot of it isn't actually lip-reading… it's just joining the dot dot dots… putting together what you expect.

DANIEL. What, guessing?

BILLY *stares at* DANIEL.

BILLY. Why aren't you nicer to her?

DANIEL. I am. I am nice.

BILLY. No, you're not.

Beat.

Why don't you like her?

DANIEL. Course I like her. I love her.

He gestures above them.

And they love her. I never thought I'd see the day.

BILLY. Yeah. Yeah, Dan.

I get it.

Pause.

DANIEL. How do you know it's the real thing?

BILLY. Why don't you want it to be the real thing?

DANIEL. I do. I do, I do.

A pause in which they look at each other. SYLVIA *comes in.*

SYLVIA. Hi.

DANIEL. Hi…!

The three of them look at each other.

Can I get you anything? Cup of tea?

(*He gestures.*) …Cup of tea?

SYLVIA.… No. It's okay.

Pause.

BILLY. I'm going up.

He makes to leave. SYLVIA *does not move.*

Are you coming up?

SYLVIA. **No.**

I'll just stay down here a bit.

BILLY. **Why?**

SYLVIA. *Just don't feel sleepy yet.*

BILLY. ... *Okay.*

Well, he's being a prick. I'm going up. See you up there.

SYLVIA. *Okay.*

BILLY *goes. A pause.*

DANIEL. ... You sure I can't get you anything?

SYLVIA. Well... What I feel like... is a 'nuit-grave', actually.

She smiles.

DANIEL. Hey...! Good knowledge of family slang!

So let's have a nuit-grave.

He gets out a packet of cigarettes.

SYLVIA. What? We can't, can we? I thought –

He hands her one.

DANIEL. Yeah, we can.

SYLVIA. Seriously?

DANIEL. New house rules. We're allowed. Honestly.

He lights two cigarettes.

SYLVIA. You *sure*?

DANIEL *nods.*

DANIEL. Billy said I had to be nice to you.

SYLVIA. What?

DANIEL. Billy said you were giving up.

Stopping.

SYLVIA. He said *you* were giving up.

DANIEL. I can't.

SYLVIA. I know how you feel.

DANIEL. Yeah. They're my friends. Utterly reliable. And they never answer back.

They smoke.

So Billy's trial went well. Evidence.

SYLVIA. 'Heavy'…?

DANIEL. Billy. Giving ev-i-dence.

SYLVIA. …. Oh, yeah! It's amazing, he got the whole of the conversation, I think they're going to convict the guy on the strength of it.

DANIEL. Great.

SYLVIA. I hope you don't think I'm – But yeah, I – I do think it's… going to be great for Billy. I think his self-esteem, you know… got a bit pounded down, and…

What?

DANIEL. What?

Beat.

SYLVIA. I don't know, you were looking at me sort of funny.

Beat.

DANIEL. So where did you guys go? Tonight?

SYLVIA. Dinner and then this drinks thing.

DANIEL. Deaf?

SYLVIA. What?

DANIEL. Was it a deaf drinks thing?

SYLVIA. Yeah.

DANIEL. He's getting very into all that stuff. Billy.

SYLVIA. Yeah…

You go through phases. Billy's still in the honeymoon phase. 'Wow, this is where I belong.'

Then it's – 'Oh God, it's always the same faces. Dramas. Gossip. Chinese whispers.'

Then – 'I'm going to withdraw.'

It is a very small world.

Beat.

DANIEL. Where are you at?

SYLVIA. 'I'm going to withdraw'…

Beat.

DANIEL. You know they all really like you. Mum… Dad… the family.

SYLVIA. Oh… do they? (*She touches her face.*)

…I wish I'd met you all when I was hearing.

DANIEL. Why?

SYLVIA. I wouldn't miss out on so much.

DANIEL. What?

SYLVIA. I don't know. The jokes. The dramas.

Beat.

DANIEL. Are you and Billy going to move in together?

SYLVIA. Yes.

DANIEL. Billy's not had a girlfriend before.

SYLVIA. He told me.

DANIEL. He sleeps with the light on.

SYLVIA. Not with me he doesn't.

They stare at each other. Suddenly DANIEL *starts, and moves to the door.*

What?

DANIEL. Shh!

He stands by the door, listening. SYLVIA *takes a step forward.*

SYLVIA. What is it?

Suddenly, DANIEL *turns around and comes back to*
SYLVIA.

DANIEL. Quick.

*He takes the cigarette from her, swiftly puts both of them out
on a saucer and throws them away.*

SYLVIA. What are you doing?!

Beat.

DANIEL. I thought I heard someone coming.

SYLVIA. I thought you said we could smoke!

Beat. They stare at each other, then start giggling. DANIEL
puts his finger to his lips.

DANIEL. Shhh…

Pause.

Don't take him away.

SYLVIA….What?

DANIEL. Don't take him away from me.

SYLVIA. I don't understand.

Beat. DANIEL *moves towards her. Then, he kisses her.*

DANIEL *and* SYLVIA *part and look at each other. Music: 'I
Wanna Be Like You' from Disney's* The Jungle Book.
Surtitles for the lyrics come up.

Scene Two

BETH *and* RUTH *are in the kitchen. Nearby,* CHRISTOPHER
*sits in an armchair with his laptop on his lap. He has his
headphones in his ears.* BETH *and* RUTH *speak in an
undertone to each other.* BETH *is tearful.* RUTH *is in the
middle of ironing sheets.*

RUTH (*indicating* CHRISTOPHER *with her head*). Well what did *he* say?

BETH. Nothing. He's completely useless. Not interested.

Beat.

I'm fed up with it.

Beat.

He's worse. Definitely worse. His stammer's coming back. He hasn't stammered since he was ten years old.

RUTH. Do you know *why* he's worse?

BETH. No. Maybe he's stopped taking his medication.

RUTH (*indicating* CHRISTOPHER *with her head*). What does he say?

BETH. What do *you* think? He's been shouting at him all week. Saying he's lazy, he should get a job, he treats the place like a hotel, that he has me running round all day after him.

RUTH. Well, he thinks we all do. (*Looking over at* CHRISTOPHER.) Can he hear us?

BETH. No. (*She is distracted by* RUTH's *ironing*.) Honeybun, there's a much better way of doing it. It'll take you for ever like that.

She takes over the ironing.

Look. What you have to do is stretch out the side of it, like this, and then…

She becomes engrossed with the ironing. RUTH *looks beadily at* CHRISTOPHER.

RUTH. Why doesn't *he* ever help? Why does he let you do everything? God.

She looks at her watch.

What time are they coming? What's it about, anyway?

BETH. I don't know, did Billy not tell you?

RUTH. No. He hasn't been around.

Beat.

Maybe he's going to tell us they're getting engaged.

BETH. Oh, I hope not. Things are hard enough for Dan already. I'm sure he wouldn't be in this state if Billy was around more to talk to him.

RUTH. I thought you wanted Billy to have his own life.

BETH. I know, but that doesn't stop me worrying about Dan.

RUTH. You know your trouble, Mum – you've got too much empathy.

BETH.... The *Guardian* want to do a feature on Billy. Expert witness. Star of the CPS...

Beat.

RUTH. Fucking hell!! Seriously?

BETH. I think that's going to be hard for Dan –

RUTH. The *Guardian*? Bloody hell.

BETH. Look. I'm only going to say this once. All of you, Dan *and* you, I include you both in this, need to swallow your egos for a second, and be pleased for Billy. All those years of you both doing well in exams and now it's his turn, it's absolutely deserved. I understand that you're competitive and it's hard for you both but you *can't* show Billy that.

RUTH. Well, that's your answer! *That's* why Dan's in a state!

BETH. No, Dan doesn't know about the *Guardian*. And please don't tell him, yet.

Sylvia told me. She's such a nice girl. Nice and funny.

RUTH (*sing-song*). Yeah, 'nice and funny', 'nice and funny', like *sick* and *tired*! The *Guardian*?! I want to *shoot* myself. Fucking hell... if only I could find my voice...

BETH. You *have* found your voice. You're a singer.

RUTH. No I'm not. I was practising the other day, I taped myself, I listened to it and I sound *awful*. I can't believe I've been going around making that noise. And now that fucking bitch from college is singing *Aida*…

BETH. Well. 'That's opera!' Exclamation mark.

RUTH. I just think, what if some people just *are* born better?

BETH. Well, some people are born better. It's true. More beautiful, or… and it's funny, when you're born with an advantage, it's a snowball thing; if you're pretty, people are nicer to you, so then you get more –

RUTH. Thanks Mum. That's really cheered me up. What about attitude, application?

BETH. No, I think either you've got it or you haven't. But –

RUTH. Great! Fucking great!

BETH. Ruth –

Suddenly, RUTH *is in tears.*

RUTH. *When* am I going to get a fucking *boyfriend*?? What is *wrong* with me?

BETH (*shocked*). Goodness me… sweetie…!

She hugs her.

There's nothing *wrong* with you… a boyfriend? Gosh… You're all so *emotional*…

RUTH. There *is* something wrong with me… and Dan… we're fucked… just look at us…

Over her shoulder, RUTH *catches sight of a small gun on the kitchen table. She pulls out of the embrace, picks it up, curiosity overriding her tears.*

Mum… what the hell is this?

BETH. A BB gun.

RUTH. A *what*?

BETH. A BB gun. Christopher bought it.

RUTH. What *for*?

BETH. The mice.

They look at each other.

He said he could shoot them with it.

RUTH. And he wonders why his son hears voices.

BETH. Yes. It's a marvel you've all turned out so sane, really.

CHRISTOPHER speaks loud and deaf from where he sits, his headphones still in his ears.

CHRISTOPHER. It doesn't work. I tried using it.

BETH and RUTH both start, guiltily.

It's pathetic. You could fire that gun directly into your own *eye* and the *gun* would be sore.

Beat. RUTH turns the gun on herself.

BETH (*anxiously*). Ruth –

RUTH *shoots herself in the chest several times. The gas propellant is at such a low ebb that the bullets drop lethargically to the floor.*

RUTH. I see. Yes. Mildly arousing.

CHRISTOPHER shuts down his laptop and gets up.

CHRISTOPHER. So.

He looks at his watch.

Where are they? Where's Daniel? The rest of us can make the effort to be here, why can't he?

BETH starts folding the sheet with RUTH. CHRISTOPHER shouts, throwing his voice.

Daniel!!

BETH. He can't hear you. (*To RUTH, re: the sheet.*) Is this a double or a single?

CHRISTOPHER (*goes off, shouting*). *Daniel!*

BETH (*shouting*). Stop *shouting* at him!

RUTH (*bitterly*). Single.

CHRISTOPHER comes back on, then, as a sudden second thought –

CHRISTOPHER (*bellowing*). *Daniel!!*

BETH (*beseechingly*). Christopher!

She passes RUTH a small laundry basket. RUTH starts to pair-up socks. BETH starts to iron another sheet.

In the moment of relative hush, CHRISTOPHER switches on the radio – a piece of music has just concluded.

COMMENTATOR.… the difference tempo can make. That, in my opinion, is simply *too* slow, meaning the burden of the melody seems to lie with the birdsong motif. Whereas in fact, the interest, one might say, *story* actually rests in the cellos, as we see thus, with a quicker tempo:

Music starts up. DANIEL comes in.

CHRISTOPHER. Where were you?

Beat.

Where *were* you?

DANIEL. Upstairs.

RUTH. Did you not hear Dad? Calling you?

DANIEL. Yes.

CHRISTOPHER. Why didn't you answer?

DANIEL. I thought it was my auditory hallucinations.

CHRISTOPHER. Oh my God. He thought it was his fucking auditory hallucinations.

BETH. Christopher –

CHRISTOPHER. Don't smoke pot! You get auditory hallucinations, don't smoke pot! Jesus!

DANIEL walks out. CHRISTOPHER looks around at BETH and RUTH.

What?

BETH. I'm not saying anything.

– All I'm saying is, he is obviously upset! If there's a bruise, don't press it.

I know you're worried –

CHRISTOPHER. I'm not worried. I'm irritated. Listen, *I* was mad in my twenties. *Everyone*'s mad in their twenties. But he shouldn't be smoking pot.

RUTH. Skunk.

BETH. It's a comforting duvet between him and the world.

CHRISTOPHER. I have never understood that argument. If he needs a comforting duvet between him and the world, then, buy a fucking duvet. Buy a duvet! Don't smoke pot.

BETH. Oh, for God's sake, Christopher, don't be so *literal*!

There is the noise of the front door.

That's them.

CHRISTOPHER (*looking at his watch*). I resent this. I've got stuff to do.

BETH. Shut up.

CHRISTOPHER (*shouting*). Daniel! They're here!

Beat.

Anyone know what it's about?

BETH *and* RUTH *shake their heads.*

RUTH. No. Sylvia just texted, saying Billy wanted to talk to us about something.

CHRISTOPHER. Yes, but what's it about? Is it about his job?

BETH. We don't know.

CHRISTOPHER. *Billy* hasn't said what it's about to anybody?

BETH *and* RUTH *shake their heads.*

Has anyone *spoken* to Billy lately?

BETH *and* RUTH *shake their heads.*

RUTH. He hasn't been *here*, somehow.

Beat.

Do you think it's something serious?

The temperature in the room changes as all three consider this possibility. They all stand and wait, looking at the door, for SYLVIA *and* BILLY *to come in. Which, after a beat, they do.*

A moment. Then –

BETH. Hello!

She gives SYLVIA *a hug.*

Did you get that piece I e-mailed you?

SYLVIA. Yeah, thanks. Really interesting.

BETH. I *thought* you'd be interested.

(*To both of them.*) Do you want a cup of tea?

SYLVIA *shakes her head.*

Billy?

BILLY *shakes his head. Silence. Surtitles start to come up, as indicated.*

How's the case going?

Why isn't Billy saying anything?

Everyone looks at BILLY *but he does not respond.*

… The case?

Billy?

SYLVIA. It's very hectic.

Beat.

… There's loads of footage and it's crucial evidence, you know, so, Billy's been at it non-stop…

BETH. It's lovely to be busy. You haven't told me anything about it yet, Billy. I want to hear all about it. I won't put it in my book, promise.

What's wrong?

Beat.

CHRISTOPHER. Well. I don't know about you, but I will have a cup of tea.

Let's open some biscuits, too. Rock and roll.

We're in a Pinter play.

He goes and starts making a cup of tea.

BETH. Great news about the *Guardian*, Billy. Sylvia told me.

Say something.

BILLY *does not respond.*

SYLVIA. The – ?

BETH (*enunciating*). *Guardian.* Wanting to – (*She gestures at* BILLY.)

SYLVIA. Yeah. Yeah. It's great.

I'm sorry.

BETH. Yes.

Sorry?

RUTH *leaves the room. Pause.*

CHRISTOPHER. Sylvia, how have you been?

Maybe she's pregnant.

BETH. Yes, how have you been?

Sorry about what?

SYLVIA. I've been fine.

CHRISTOPHER. Good. And the charity?

Her breasts look bigger.

SYLVIA. Great. Thank you.

RUTH and DANIEL both come in.

DANIEL. Hi.

SYLVIA. Hi.

Everyone stands around, awkwardly. A pause, then –

BETH. So. What's all this about?

What's all this about?

Billy?

A pause. BILLY looks at SYLVIA. She looks back at him. Then, BILLY starts to sign. No surtitles. The signing goes on for a while. Finally, SYLVIA turns to the family.

SYLVIA. Billy says that he's decided to stop talking to you. He thinks you should all learn sign.

Pause.

He says… he's spent his life trying to understand you and now he thinks you should try to understand him.

Beat.

BETH. Billy…

Billy…

CHRISTOPHER. I'm sorry. Did I hear that right? Did she just say what I thought she said?

BILLY starts signing again. The family wait, looking at him. SYLVIA waits until BILLY has finished. Then turns to the family.

SYLVIA. He says, this was the only way you were ever going to take any notice.

BETH turns to BILLY.

BETH. But, Billy –

BILLY signs to SYLVIA, who watches. She turns to the family.

SYLVIA. He says that when you all learn sign, then he'll talk to you again.

Beat.

CHRISTOPHER. Why?

This is because of her.

BETH. I think we need to try to understand –

No, it isn't.

Is this to do with the job? I mean, Billy, are you stressed, or, depressed, or –

BILLY *'interrupts', signing to* SYLVIA, *'No.' Then he continues. This time she starts to talk simultaneously, with only a short lag between sign and speech. (NB. At first* SYLVIA *does not overlay any 'emotions' on what she says, her tone is simply that of concentration – on giving the most accurate translation possible. Emotions start to surface as the scene progresses.)*

SYLVIA. The bland level of conversation. 'How's work?' 'How are you?' You never explain your arguments. You're all laughing about something and I have to say 'What?' 'What?' 'What?' 'Oh nothing. It was about a book.' I'm tired of saying 'what what what' all the time.

Beat.

CHRISTOPHER. You mean you're tired of being deaf.

BILLY *signs.* SYLVIA *speaks in tandem.*

SYLVIA. No. That's not what I'm saying.

CHRISTOPHER. Well, that's what *I'm* saying.

BILLY *signs.* SYLVIA *translates.*

SYLVIA. I don't have to feel deaf.

BETH. But we *do* explain – !

Do we explain?

BILLY *signs.* SYLVIA *simultaneously translates.*

SYLVIA. No, you don't. I've had to fit in with you. I've waited. I've waited and waited. I keep thinking, 'I'll wait and you'll come to me' but you never do. You can't be bothered.

Pause.

BETH. Sylvia, has Billy talked to you about this?

Is *this because of her?*

SYLVIA. A bit. Not much.

BETH. No, that's okay. I understand.

I don't understand.

SYLVIA. He just wanted me to translate… I don't… This isn't me.

BILLY *starts to sign.* SYLVIA *hesitates and does not translate.*

RUTH. What?

DANIEL. What did he say?

SYLVIA. Sorry… it's… erm…

BILLY *signs a bit more.* SYLVIA, *reluctantly, translates.*

… Sylvia understands the way I feel. Because she's told me how she feels and it's how I feel. A second-class citizen.

Beat.

BETH. Billy, put yourself in our position –

I tried –

BILLY *'interrupts' in sign.* SYLVIA *translates.*

SYLVIA. No. You put yourself in mine.

Beat.

CHRISTOPHER. Well. This is extremely fucking interesting. Isn't it.

Well, was I right, or was I right? About the deaf community? Folks?

Pause.

BETH. Billy, I'm so sorry –

They told me not to. We agreed. He said –

CHRISTOPHER. What are you apologising for?

BETH. Because it upsets me to hear this!

We did the wrong thing!

Beat. BILLY *starts to sign again.* SYLVIA *translates.*

SYLVIA. When I got depressed, at school, you said you would learn sign if I wanted. But you didn't.

BETH. But you didn't want –

BILLY *signs.*

SYLVIA. No. You just didn't want to hear it.

BETH *speaks slowly, haltingly, and her surtitles follow suit.*

BETH. But, Billy…

It was…

… you adapted…

He was… Dad was…

… so well that…

We were arguing a lot at the time.

BILLY *is still signing.* SYLVIA *translates.*

SYLVIA. I've never lost my temper. And you made promises. 'We'll learn sign.' You never did.

BETH. Because you adapted so well, Billy. Don't you see? You were amazing. When I taught you –

I did my best.

SYLVIA *interrupts.*

SYLVIA. You had a long time to do something. And you didn't do anything.

Silence.

BILLY *starts to sign again.* SYLVIA *looks uncertain. Instead of translating,* SYLVIA *signs back to* BILLY. *In turn,* BILLY *signs back to her.* SYLVIA *vehemently signs back to him. The family wait for as long as they can bear, then –*

RUTH. What??

Beat.

SYLVIA. Sorry, I was just… I was saying… it doesn't matter what I was saying.

DANIEL. What?

SYLVIA. I said –

CHRISTOPHER. No, what did *Billy* say?

DANIEL. Don't argue with it, just translate it!

Beat.

SYLVIA. Am I not important to you?

Beat.

RUTH (*baffled*). What?

SYLVIA. … I mean, that's what he said.

BETH *is near tears.*

BETH. Sweetie pie, what a stupid question.

Of course you are. We love you.

I love you.

BILLY *stands, signs vehemently, pointing at* CHRISTOPHER. SYLVIA *translates.*

SYLVIA. Then why can't you be bothered?

(*Re:* CHRISTOPHER.) He bothered to learn Chinese.

RUTH. Because none of us can be bothered with *any* of us! That's this family. We're all egotists.

We get it from him.

BETH. Fuck you!

RUTH. Well, we are!

CHRISTOPHER. No, *no* one gets special treatment. You think everyone is always included anyway? It's bollocks! Half the time the conversation is over Ruth's head.

RUTH. It's true, it is.

CHRISTOPHER. And as a matter of fact, it's ironic you think of yourself as a second-class citizen because I think you're the cleverest of my children.

Or I did, until you started all this melodramatic shit.

(*Generally.*) I mean, are we really going to take all this *seriously*?

BETH. Yes.

If you hadn't had that affair with –

CHRISTOPHER. No!

My God, it's like he's coming out or something. You sure you don't want to tell us you're gay, as well?

BILLY *signs.* SYLVIA *turns to them.*

SYLVIA. This is the first time you've ever listened to me properly and it's because I'm not speaking.

Pause.

CHRISTOPHER. Look, the reason we didn't learn sign wasn't because we couldn't be bothered, it was out of principle. Out of principle, we didn't want to make you part of a minority world.

I feel completely unapologetic.

BETH. Yes.

Yes, you're good at that.

BILLY *starts to sign.* CHRISTOPHER *turns impatiently to* SYLVIA.

CHRISTOPHER. Go on.

SYLVIA is distressed.

SYLVIA.... This is... this is... wrong, I can't, I... I feel like I
    shouldn't be...

BETH. Just tell us what he's saying!

SYLVIA.... When I learnt sign and Sylvia took me and I met
    people – I didn't want to leave. I fit. I belong with them.
    When I leave – I'm alone again.

I'm not hearing so stop pretending I am.

Beat.

CHRISTOPHER. I'm sorry.

I'm not saying sorry.

I find this urge to conform deeply, deeply depressing. I've
    said it before and I'll say it again –

***I mean, what's the subtext here? Really? What is this really
    all about?***

BILLY *starts to sign and* BETH *interrupts* CHRISTOPHER.

BETH. Can we please shut up and listen to what Billy has to say!

BILLY *continues to sign. Beat.*

SYLVIA *translates.*

SYLVIA. If anywhere's a closed bloody ghetto it's this bloody
    house. Conventionally... unconventional. Kimonos. You think
    we're not part of any community, that's because we're our
    own... totally bonkers... hermetically sealed... community.
    'No hawkers, no traders, and no one who doesn't know who
    (*Hesitantly, as she watches the name be finger-spelled.*) Dv...
    o... řák is.' And no one's allowed to leave. I'm fed up with it.

Pause.

RUTH. Well... that's probably fair.

BETH. But you're part of it, Billy, you're part of it.

BILLY *signs. He finds it difficult to describe what he wants to say and there are false starts which* SYLVIA *translates, hesitantly.*

SYLVIA. No, I – when – I – I'm not. I'm not part of – because – it's – I'm your mascot. That's not part.

DANIEL. Billy, you never knew any deaf people. You didn't like it. You hated that other deaf boy at school. You went to one deaf do and you hated it. You said you had nothing in common.

I was bullied and so were you. You said you didn't feel 'deaf'.

SYLVIA *turns, signs to* BILLY, *questioningly. He signs back, shaking his head.*

More signing between SYLVIA *and* BILLY.

(*To* BILLY.) You *did*. You said that no one listened to anyone else. You said that they didn't seem to realise conversation is about taking turns, not just talking all the time.

Have you told her that?

RUTH. Sounds like us.

DANIEL. Shut up. And that they *ignored* you when they found out you didn't sign. (*To* SYLVIA.) Didn't he tell you that?

BILLY *signs to* SYLVIA. *She signs back. He signs back to her.*

SYLVIA. He says all that changed after he learnt sign.

Pause. BILLY *signs.* SYLVIA *turns to them, awkwardly.*

I don't feel like I'm part of this family. I feel more like I'm part of Sylvia's.

The family all burst out at this point, all talking at once. Their lines come up, very fast, with simultaneous surtitles as in an operatic quartet but with additions, as shown. The surtitles finally end with DANIEL's 'score':

CHRISTOPHER. / Oh, for God's *sake*! This is bullshit!

– Oh for God's sake *This is bullshit*

sentence fragment

BETH. / With all due respect, Billy, we've known you a little *longer* than you've known Sylvia's family and I think you should realise – !

– With all due respect Billy we've known you a little **longer** *than you've known Sylvia's family and I think you should realise Declarative IMPERATIVE.*

RUTH. / Since when? Since when? Since I listened to you for hours going on about whether you had a chance with Sylvia or not?

– Since when Since when Since I listened to you for hours going on about whether you had a chance with Sylvia or not **Interrogatory???**

DANIEL. / This is a fucking blank cheque of *guilt* that we're meant to fucking *sign* for you all of a sudden?

– This is a fucking blank cheque of guilt that we're meant to fucking sign for you all of a sudden rhetorical question direct indirect object possessive possessive pronoun possessive apostrophe possessive pronoun, noun, noun, no.

BILLY *tears out his hearing aids and the noise suddenly cuts out into a loud underwater hum – what a deaf person might hear – and the family are left mouthing silently and vehemently with the last of* DANIEL's *surtitles coming up.* BILLY *and* SYLVIA *simultaneously sign and speak their words to each other.*

BILLY. *Why do you keep looking at him?*

SYLVIA. *Who?*

BILLY. *Him. Why do you keep looking at him?*

SYLVIA. *I'm not.*

BILLY. *You are.*

SYLVIA. *Billy, stop it. Stop it.*

BILLY. *Stop what?*

SYLVIA. *Stop being jealous. You're being paranoid. Stop.*

Just as suddenly, the hum cuts out and we can hear the family again. DANIEL is getting upset. For the first time, we hear DANIEL's stutter start to surface. The surtitles fade up and down, slowly; single words.

DANIEL. Why is this – ha – ha – happening? When – d – did you start – ?

Why

Pause. Then BILLY signs. SYLVIA translates.

SYLVIA. When I brought Sylvia round.

Sylvia

DANIEL. What *about* when you brought S – Sylvia round?

When

Beat. BILLY signs, SYLVIA translates, awkwardly.

SYLVIA. You all tried harder with her than you've ever tried with me. Why?

Try

The surtitles 'flatline' –

BILLY *is staring at* DANIEL. *Everyone is at a loss.*

DANIEL. You've got it so wrong.

Pause. BILLY signs, slowly and clearly. SYLVIA translates, close to tears.

SYLVIA. I'm leaving you.

BILLY *signs some more.*

I don't want you any more. I don't need you any more.

Finally, RUTH *speaks.*

RUTH. Billy… don't you remember Mum teaching you to speak? She spent hours with you.

DANIEL *is also near tears.*

DANIEL. We love you most, you idiot, we love you most.

BILLY *and* DANIEL *stare at each other.* BILLY *does not speak. He turns and leaves.* SYLVIA *looks at them, lost for words.*

(*To* SYLVIA.) Can't you explain that to him?

SYLVIA *says nothing. Pause. The family say nothing.* CHRISTOPHER *goes and wordlessly puts in his headphones again.* BETH *starts to cry.* RUTH *goes over to her and hugs her.* DANIEL *goes over to the table. He picks up* BILLY'*s hearing aids and holds them cupped in his hands. He stares down at them.* SYLVIA *stands, at a loss. Music: 'Try (Just a Little Bit Harder)' by Janis Joplin.*

Scene Three

SYLVIA'*s flat.* BILLY *is watching some black-and-white CCTV footage: two men talking in a car park. He is taking notes.* SYLVIA *comes in.*

SYLVIA. Billy –

BILLY *continues to take notes.*

Billy.

She taps him on the arm.

Billy!

He looks up.

I'm not going to come tonight.

BILLY *does not respond – he is looking back at the television.* SYLVIA *tries to take the piece of paper from him.* BILLY *lifts it out of reach.*

Billy – listen to me – !

SYLVIA *stands between* BILLY *and the television. Watches it a moment. Turns to* BILLY.

BILLY (*re: the paper/CCTV*). **It's boring.**

SYLVIA. Billy –

She makes a grab for the remote. BILLY *gets there first.* SYLVIA *makes unsuccessful attempts to get the remote.*

Look… pause it… *pause it…*

SYLVIA *finally manages to grab the remote from* BILLY. *She pauses the footage.*

BILLY. **What's wrong?**

SYLVIA. **Nothing.**

Beat.

BILLY. **What did you want to say to me?**

SYLVIA. There are carol singers outside.

BILLY. **Well, they've come to the wrong place, haven't they.**

SYLVIA. **Billy, I'm not going to come tonight.**

BILLY. **To the drinks?**

She nods.

Why?

SYLVIA. I just… don't want to.

Beat.

It doesn't mean you can't go. I'm not stopping you.

BILLY. But why?

SYLVIA. Because…

Beat.

I don't know why.

BILLY *makes to sign something but she 'interrupts'.*

– Because it's always the same faces. Everyone smiling the whole time, in your face. It's so competitive. Who's the best storyteller. Who's got the highest status. By the end of the night, I'm all faked out, my *cheeks* hurt.

Beat.

BILLY. *Say it in sign.*

SYLVIA. *I can't.*

There's no empathy. 'You're going deaf – so what? We're all deaf.' You're not allowed to be depressed about it. 'You're depressed? I'll tell you a joke.' You've got to act like you've won a competition. (*She simultaneously signs and speaks.*) 'Oh congratulations! You're *deaf*!'

BILLY. … So what do you want me to do?

It was you that… wanted me to…

SYLVIA. I know…

Beat.

BILLY. *What's happened?*

SYLVIA. Nothing.

Suddenly, she takes his notes off him. She looks at them. She turns, and starts the tape again. A pause while the tape plays, silently. She watches the flickery black-and-white CCTV for a moment. Then she looks down at the paper.

(*Reading aloud from the paper.*) 'The gear's got to go by Thursday. We're trying to shift thirty-five of them. Pete's driving the lorry…'

But you can't see his face.

BILLY. *You can.*

SYLVIA. *You can't.*

They watch a little longer.

SYLVIA *looks at the piece of paper again.*

How much of this do you make up?

BILLY. I don't make anything up.

Beat. He makes the inverted commas in the air.

'Speech reading inevitably involves inference from incomplete information.'

Beat.

I can tell something has happened so tell me.

Pause.

SYLVIA. I got that weird sideways look today… you know?

My voice must be going flat. I can't hear my voice any more.

I've lost the last little bit. I had a little bit left, and now I can feel that it's gone. I can *hear* that it's gone. No one told me it was going to be this *noisy* going deaf… It's this buzz… this roar and outside – it's all – black.

BILLY. *But you can sign.*

SYLVIA. But most people who can sign are… deaf. So it only works with… the circle… of people… you can talk to… just gets smaller.

BILLY. It's not that small. The circle.

You're not telling me what it is.

SYLVIA. *And you're not telling me. What have you done?*

She holds the paper up. They stare at each other. Abruptly, SYLVIA turns her back on BILLY.

BILLY. *Look at me.*

He stamps his foot on the floor.

Look at me!

He grabs SYLVIA. SYLVIA pulls away from him.

Tell me what it is!!

SYLVIA. Okay!

…Sometimes I feel like… they are different.

Beat.

BILLY. *Who are different?*

SYLVIA. *You know. They are.*

BILLY. *Who's 'they'?*

The…? (BILLY*'s hand creeps to his ear to make the sign for
'deaf' – but he doesn't complete it.*)

They stare at each other. SYLVIA *nods, slowly.*

SYLVIA. *Some* of them… there's a compromise. A
simplification. A… literalness. As people.

BILLY. That's an ugly word.

SYLVIA. What? 'Literalness'?

BILLY. … Am I 'different'?

SYLVIA. No. You're… different.

BILLY. *This is just because… you're panicking. You're
panicking.*

Beat.

SYLVIA. I want to talk about your trial.

I don't want to talk about this any more.

BILLY. I don't want to talk about my trial.

BILLY *turns his back on her. Then he spins round.*

Who?

SYLVIA. *What do you mean, 'who'?*

BILLY. *Who have you met?*

SYLVIA. I haven't 'met' anyone, Billy! You're like your
mother, putting all the clues in afterwards!

BILLY (*vehemently*). *Then why? Why did you stop going to
your lip-reading classes?*

SYLVIA. Because it was *depressing*. It was a self-help group
full of miserable people losing a massive part of their lives
and I was one of them, getting that deaf frown on my face,
that my brother got, my brain just *hurting* because you *never*
get time off from it –

BILLY. *I know what it's like being deaf!*

SYLVIA. But you don't know what it's like *going* deaf! You
don't!

SYLVIA *starts to simultaneously sign and speak*.

I just keep thinking, 'Am I different? Am I different? Am I
different? Am I turning into somebody different?' I'm
becoming a miserable person. I feel like I'm losing my
personality… can't even be ironic any more… I love being
ironic… I feel *stupid*… when I lose something in the house I
have to put my hearing aids in to *look* for it…

I have these dreams… when I'm talking on the phone again.
And I can hear perfectly. It's all so clear…

I don't know who I am any more… I'm going deaf.

*We hear the faint noise of the carol singers. They are singing
'And He Shall Purify' from Handel's* Messiah, *and their
singing builds in volume to the end of the scene.* BILLY *also
signs and speaks simultaneously.*

BILLY. Look, Sylvia, you can turn into a dull, deaf person,
'*listening*', all the time, not saying anything, it's like being
blind with a white stick. I've done that, I did it at school and
university and after. When all my friends were girls who told
me about their problems with their boyfriends while I
thought, 'I'm here. I'm free.' And got confused and
depressed. Or you can take the risk, you can think, 'I'm
going to jump from one guess to the other, why should they
be the ones to show off and tell all the stories?' (*He reads
from the paper.*) 'Thirty-five computers. We'll make a killing
if we can just bring in the stuff in time. We're made.'

Beat.

SYLVIA.…*What have you done?*

BILLY. *I haven't done anything. Nothing that no one else does.*

Think everyone knows what they're doing? You make an educated guess. Use your imagination. *Everyone* is deaf. We're one of the crowd.

You can tell who's guilty. Sometimes just by how they react.

Pause.

SYLVIA. Billy, you can't do that.

BILLY. Why not?

SYLVIA. You're just… It's writing your own story.

BILLY (*flatly*). Why shouldn't I write my own story.

SYLVIA. They put people in prison on that evidence.

BILLY. Lip-reading is only ever part of the evidence. You add it to other things. Like in real life.

SYLVIA. A trial *is* real life.

Beat.

BILLY. I did it for you.

I've told you the truth, now you tell me the truth.

Pause.

Your hands are shaking.

SYLVIA. It's my tremor.

They don't when I'm drunk.

BILLY. Same as Dan and his voices. Something happened with you and him. Didn't it.

Beat.

Also, you get very very good at spotting when somebody's being fake.

SYLVIA. You're being paranoid.

BILLY. I took a risk when I met you. I bluffed… But you fell in love with them, not me.

SYLVIA. No. I didn't.

BILLY. I left them for you. Are you leaving me?

> *Pause.*

> *Please, tell me in sign.*

SYLVIA. *Go back to them. They love you.*

BILLY. *I don't want them, I want you.*

SYLVIA (*speaks and signs, vehemently*). *Not everything in my life can be deaf.*

> BILLY *claps his hands over his eyes.*

BILLY. No. No. No. No. No.

> *Music: 'Cry Baby' by Janis Joplin.*

Scene Four

SYLVIA, DANIEL *and* RUTH *stand in the kitchen. Silence.*

RUTH. Why are you here?

SYLVIA. He's being investigated.

> DANIEL *winces.*

What?

RUTH. Nothing. He gets these voices. That was a voice.

> *Pause.*

SYLVIA. What did the voice say?

> DANIEL*'s stutter momentarily emerges.*

DANIEL. 'You're f-f-f – ucking useless.'

Is he –

> *He cannot complete the sentence.* RUTH *does so for him.*

RUTH. Is he going to come back?

SYLVIA. I don't know.

RUTH. Is he going to go to prison?

SYLVIA. It wasn't all wrong. He got two hundred and thirty-six words right.

DANIEL. How…

Again, RUTH *completes his sentence.*

RUTH. How many did he get wrong?

SYLVIA. Well, they don't say 'wrong'. They say 'added'.

RUTH. How many words did he add?

SYLVIA. Approximately one thousand, eight hundred and fifty.

The audio for one of the tapes turned up.

A policeman made a transcript and checked it against what Billy had. It didn't match Billy's transcript.

Beat. DANIEL*'s stutter emerges more strongly.*

DANIEL. W – hy d – id he…

He pauses, takes a breath.

SYLVIA. What is it?

RUTH. His stammer's come back.

DANIEL *takes another breath.*

DANIEL. Why did he do it?

SYLVIA. I don't know. He wouldn't tell me.

We're not together any more.

DANIEL *winces again, takes his head in his hands.*

What?

…What?

RUTH. Leave him alone.

DANIEL (*to* SYLVIA). I can't hear what you're saying. It's talking louder than you are.

It's just talking over you, every time you talk. Interrupting.

SYLVIA. Why?

RUTH. Who cares why. Leave him alone.

SYLVIA. What does it say?

DANIEL. Fuck off, shut up, I don't want to hear.

Beat.

Can't you hear it?

Pause.

SYLVIA. What happens when you answer back?

RUTH. He doesn't. Stop talking about it, it makes it worse.

Pause.

Why don't you go?

SYLVIA (*to* DANIEL). I came to see you.

DANIEL *winces again.*

What did it say?

DANIEL. 'Tell her to fuck off.'

SYLVIA. Why did you kiss me?

DANIEL. It was a mistake.

SYLVIA. Why?

RUTH. Stop it. You're upsetting him.

SYLVIA. I'm talking to him, not you. Why did you do it?

DANIEL*'s stutter emerges again but he overrides it.*

DANIEL. – B-because… I didn't want him to leave.

He winces.

SYLVIA. If you tell me what the voice is saying I'll talk to it.

Pause.

DANIEL. I can't.

I can't say yes. I can't.

Scene Five

BILLY *and* DANIEL *are standing in the kitchen.* DANIEL*'s stutter emerges periodically throughout the scene on the odd word. Otherwise he speaks normally.*

BILLY. Do they know about it?

DANIEL. No.

BILLY. Does anyone know?

DANIEL. No. Mum does. Sylvia told her.

Pause.

What happened?

BILLY. Your stammer has come back.

DANIEL. Yeah.

It came back after you left.

Beat.

How are you?

BILLY. You know what I think? When you say to someone for the first time, 'I miss you', it actually means, 'I love you.'

I think we're going to get back together.

DANIEL. ….That's great. Billy. I'm so pleased.

BILLY. Yeah.

She said I had to talk to you.

Pause.

DANIEL. You know… You don't have to talk about it.

BILLY. It's all right.

Beat.

DANIEL. You… made stuff up… when you looked at those
     tapes.

BILLY. Sometimes.

DANIEL. You *invented*.

BILLY. I *guessed*. Sometimes. Sometimes not.

It was what they wanted to hear.

Pause.

It's easy. You just imagine what it's like to be the people.
You know what the story might be. You put yourself in their
place. Like Mum does, really.

It was fun, thinking what they might be saying.

The weird thing is, I think I was usually right even when I
was just guessing.

DANIEL. How come?

BILLY. Because I'm good at guessing.

I know what happened with you and Sylvia.

Pause.

DANIEL. Did they convict people on that evidence?

BILLY. Yes. Sometimes.

Why did you do it?

Pause.

DANIEL.…. Why did you do it?

I don't know.

BILLY.… I don't know.

Pause.

They might not prosecute.

DANIEL. How come?

BILLY. Cos… on that one… even though I was guessing… the gist was actually right.

Silence.

How's Ruth?

DANIEL. Okay. Still single, but…

BILLY. How's Mum's novel going?

DANIEL. She's blocked.

BILLY. Why?

DANIEL. Dunno.

Pause.

BILLY. How are your voices?

DANIEL. It's weird… they're kind of… familiar. I'm getting used to them.

Pause. When DANIEL next speaks his stutter is so bad, it is rather like BILLY's fragmenting speech when his aids were running down. His speech is surtitled.

We don't mind why you did it, Billy.

We don't mind why you did it.

They don't mind. No one minds.

They don't mind. No one minds.

We miss you.

We miss you.

SYLVIA *comes in.* DANIEL *tries to say 'hold my hand' to* BILLY, *but fails, the stutter won't let him.*

Please…

H – my h – h –

H –

H –

He gives up, simply holds out his hand. The gesture is surtitled.

Please, hold my hand.

BILLY *does not move, does not take* DANIEL*'s hand. They look at each other.* BETH, CHRISTOPHER *and* RUTH *come in.*

BETH…. Billy…

BETH *goes over and hugs* BILLY, *hard.*

CHRISTOPHER…. Old chap…

CHRISTOPHER *touches him on the shoulder.* RUTH *hugs him. They all part and look at each other.* SYLVIA *stands slightly apart. After a pause,* DANIEL *speaks.*

DANIEL. I want to…

What's the sign for love?

BILLY. What?

DANIEL *starts to try and speak, but again the stutter stops him.*

DANIEL. What's the – s –

What –

Wh –

For –

BILLY…. What?

Slowly, DANIEL*'s words turn to improvised signs as the stutter prevents him from speaking.*

DANIEL. What's th – (*He slowly finger-spells.*) *S-I-G-N* for – (*He puts his fist to his chest, he mouths 'love'.*)

BILLY *signs*.

BILLY. *Love.*

This is two crossed arms in front of the chest. DANIEL *makes the sign back, crossing his arms in front of his chest. It looks like he is miming being in a straitjacket. He steps towards* BILLY *and they hug each other,* DANIEL *wrapping his arms around him so that they cross around his back, still in the sign for 'love'. The family watch, silently. Music: 'Humming Chorus' from* Madame Butterfly, *one minute in. Fade to black.*

The End.

A Nick Hern Book

Tribes first published in Great Britain as a paperback original in 2010 by
Nick Hern Books, 14 Larden Road, London W3 7ST, in association with
the Royal Court Theatre, London

Tribes copyright © 2010 Nina Raine

Nina Raine has asserted her right to be identified as the author of this work

Cover image: Andrew Archer
Cover design: Ned Hoste, 2H

Typeset by Nick Hern Books, London
Printed in the UK by CPI Bookmarque, Croydon, Surrey

A CIP catalogue record for this book is available from the British Library

ISBN   978 1 84842 121 9

Mixed Sources

Product group from well-managed
forests and other controlled sources
FSC www.fsc.org Cert no. TT-COC-002227
© 1996 Forest Stewardship Council